GOVERNMENT AND INDUSTRY

Government and Industry

THE PROVISION OF FINANCIAL ASSISTANCE TO INDUSTRY AND ITS CONTROL

by

GABRIELE GANZ
Reader in Law, University of Southampton

PROFESSIONAL BOOKS
1977

Published in 1977 by Professional Books Limited,
Milton Trading Estate, Abingdon, Oxon,
typeset by Inforum Limited, Portsmouth, and
printed and bound by Billing & Sons Limited, Guildford

ISBN Hardback 0 903486 34 2

PREFACE

Government assistance to industry is not a new phenomenon but due to the economic situation it has escalated in recent times. This development gives rise to great ideological controversy about public ownership but it also raises the constitutional issue of public accountability with which this book is concerned. It examines the diverse mechanisms and procedures by which billions of pounds of public money are dispensed by Ministers and independent agencies and the controls and safeguards to which they are subject. It further deals with the problem of how to hold the recipients of this money accountable to the Government, Parliament and the public. This shows that Company law does not facilitate the public accountability of limited companies. Even more difficult is the problem of how to reconcile the aims of a commercial company with the purposes of the welfare state. An examination of the constitutional issues does seem to show that mixed enterprises should be treated by analogy to the public rather than the private sector of industry.

GABRIELE GANZ

18th February 1977

CONTENTS

LIST OF SELECT COMMITTEE REPORTS

PUBLIC ACCOUNTS COMMITTEE

H.C. 183 (1963-4)
H.C. 571 (1966-7)
H.C. 647 (1966-7)
H.C. 192 (1967-8)
H.C. 314 (1967-8)
H.C. 185-I, 276-I, 362 (1968-9)
H.C. 166-I, 265-I, 297 (1969-70)
H.C. 300-I, 375-I, 537 (1970-71)
H.C. 447 (1971-2)

H.C. 335 (1972-3)
H.C. 303 (1974)
H.C. 304 (1974)
H.C. 374 (1974-5)
H.C. 502 (1974-5)
H.C. 334 (1975-6)
H.C. 556 (1975-6)
H.C. 584 (1975-6)

ESTIMATES AND EXPENDITURE COMMITTEES

H.C. 229 (1962-3)	Administration of the Local Employment Act, 1960
H.C. 42 (1963-4)	Transport Aircraft
H.C. 347 (1971-2)	Public Money in the Private Sector
H.C. 21 (1973-4)	Wages and Conditions of African Workers employed by British firms in South Africa (Minutes of Evidence)
H.C. 85 (1973-4)	Regional Development Incentives (Minutes of Evidence — H.C. 327 (1972-3) and H.C. 85-I (1973-4))
H.C. 617 (1974-5)	Motor Vehicle Industry
H.C. 299 (1975-6)	Report on White Paper 'Public Expenditure to 1979-80'
H.C. 596-I (1975-6)	Public Expenditure on Chrysler U.K. Ltd. (Minutes of Evidence — H.C. 104 (1975-6))

SELECT COMMITTEE ON NATIONALISED INDUSTRIES

H.C. 298 (1967-8)	The Committee's Order of Reference
H.C. 371 (1967-8)	Ministerial Control of Nationalised Industries
H.C. 65 (1973-4)	Capital Investment Procedures
H.C. 345 (1974-5)	Nationalised Industries and the Exploitation of North Sea Oil and Gas
H.C. 472 (1975-6)	Cable and Wireless Ltd.

Select Committee on Science and Technology

Scottish Affairs Committee

TABLE OF STATUTES

INTRODUCTION

THE line between the private and the public sector of industry is becoming increasingly blurred. Planning agreements are only the latest in a long series of developments which bring the Government and private industry closer together. But the biggest factor in blurring the line has been the use of the limited company device for public purposes. The nationalised industries were created by statute but they also own all or part of the shares in subsidiary companies formed under the Companies Act. The mechanism of the limited company whose shares are wholly owned by the Government was used to nationalise Rolls-Royce and Upper Clyde Shipbuilders. This method of nationalisation has profound effects on the relationship between the firm and Government and Parliament. The Government may also acquire all or some of the shares of existing companies in return for financial assistance, a process which has been accelerating as more and more firms ask for Government aid and which will receive even more impetus with the creation of the National Enterprise Board. Government assistance may also be in the form of grants, loans or contracts of various kinds but all these methods raise similar questions of public accountability for the expenditure of public money.

Public accountability arises in two stages — accountability for the granting of aid and for its receipt. Accountability for the granting of aid can be divided into prior approval or scrutiny and *ex post facto* control. The former will primarily depend on the statutory provisions under which assistance is provided which may vary from the passing of a special Act to an administrative decision by a Government Department or by an independent body such as the National Enterprise Board. The *ex post facto* control over the giving of aid is mainly Parliamentary and closely intertwined with the accountability of the recipient of assistance, i.e. the firm to whom public money is allocated by the Government Department or agency.

Accountability of the recipient firm depends less on the form in which aid is given, e.g. shares or loans, as on the different methods of monitoring which are employed, such as appointment of Government directors, obtaining of information and control over management. Government Departments have hitherto preferred monitoring information to interfering in management and it remains to be seen whether the National Enterprise Board will follow suit. So far as Parliamentary accountability is concerned control depends on which instrument can be employed. Only Ministers can be asked Parliamentary Questions and not on all matters, but some Select Committees summon before them not only civil servants and Ministers but those in charge of private firms. The same mechanisms are used to hold to account Government Departments and independent bodies for dispensing public aid and to oversee their monitoring of these funds. There is, however, an important difference between the accountability of Government Departments, whose accounts are audited by the Comptroller and Auditor General, and the nationalised industries, who are accountable to the Select Committee on Nationalised Industries, and limited companies wholly or partly owned by the Government, which are subject to neither control. The Nationalised Industries Committee has concerned itself particularly with attempting to reconcile public accountability and profitability by clarifying the relationship between Ministers and the industries and urging compensation for the undertaking of unprofitable social obligations. These problems have hardly been recognised in the case of firms partly or wholly owned by the Government. The creation of the National Enterprise Board, which will act as a holding company for most of these firms, will again accelerate the need to face these issues. For the conflict between profitability and social obligations has now invaded the private sector.

CHAPTER ONE

THE PROVISION OF FINANCIAL ASSISTANCE TO INDUSTRY — THE ROLE OF PARLIAMENT

UNDER this heading the different ways in which public money may be provided for the private sector will be examined from the point of view of the decision-making process. This may range from the passing of a special Act at one end of the scale to the allocation of a Government contract at the other. In form these decisions are very different but in fact they are both Government decisions which may be reached in similar ways.[1] When looking at the formal legal framework it is, therefore, necessary to bear in mind the political reality. It is nevertheless convenient to use the legal framework as a method of classification.

SPECIAL ACTS

Since the passing of the Local Employment Acts 1960-1972 and the Industry Acts 1972 and 1975, which confer wide discretionary powers to provide assistance to industry, it is only rarely necessary now to pass special legislation to authorise aid for a particular industry or project. A good illustration of this is the reorganisation of the cotton industry in comparison with that of the wool textile industry. In the case of cotton two Acts were passed in 1948[2] and 1959[3] to authorise the payment of grants for modernisation and compensation for the elimination of excess capacity in accordance with plans approved by the Board of Trade or schemes made by the Cotton Board. A similar scheme for the wool textile industry was made under s.8 of the Industry Act 1972 and announced to the House of Commons by the Minister for Industrial Development.[4] That section does not specifically authorise the payment of compensation for scrapping equipment but this was made a condition for obtaining assistance. Thus in 1973 purely administrative measures could provide the assistance which needed legislation at an earlier date.

---

[1] This point is admirably made by Daintith, [1974] J.B.L, 9, 15.
[2] Cotton Spinning (Re-equipment Subsidy) Act 1948.
[3] Cotton Industry Act 1959.
[4] 860 H.C. Deb., col. 715 (July 19, 1973) and 887 H.C. Deb., col. 212, Written Answers (February 27, 1975).

The Fort William Pulp and Paper Mills Act 1963 was also necessitated because of a gap in legislation. As the Minister explained on the Second Reading of the Bill,[5] the Local Employment Acts were not appropriate in view of the amount of assistance required (£10 million) relative to the number of jobs likely to be provided.

The proposed construction of the Channel Tunnel, which was later abandoned,[6] needed special legislation not just because of the financial assistance provided by the Government[7] but to authorise construction of the Tunnel.[8]

In the case of Concorde legislation was needed to give the Government authority to finance production losses which do not fall under the provisions of the Civil Aviation Act 1949. This authority was provided by the Industrial Expansion Act 1968, s.8, as extended by the Concorde Aircraft Act 1973.

The Civil Aviation Act 1949 also had to be amended to enable the Government to acquire Rolls-Royce Ltd. as s.1 prohibited the Minister from producing aircraft. The Rolls-Royce (Purchase) Act 1971 not only made provision for this but also authorised expenditure for the acquisition of the undertaking. A similar amendment of the Civil Aviation Act to enable the Government to acquire Beagle Aircraft Ltd. was made in s.12 of the Industrial Expansion Act 1968 but s.12 did not give authority for the expenditure of money for this purpose. This was provided through the Appropriation Act. Similarly, there was no legislation other than the Appropriation Act to authorise the expenditure of money for acquiring a shareholding in Cammell Laird Shipbuilders Ltd.[9] However, the Public Accounts Committee have criticised the setting up of a body incorporated under the Companies Act to carry on activities on behalf of the Government without specific legislation.[10] The Comptroller and Auditor General pointed out that such a self-financing body would be removed from normal Parliamentary control and that specific legislation gave Parliament the opportunity to prescribe financial controls.[11] The problems of exercising control over companies incorporated under the Companies Act which are wholly

---

[5] 675 H.C. Deb., col. 1383 (April 10, 1963).
[6] Abandonment was announced to the House of Commons on January 20, 1975 (884 H.C. Deb., col. 1021) and led to an adjournment debate under S.O.9 later that evening (*ibid.*, col. 1094).
[7] In the form of guarantees.
[8] Channel Tunnel (Initial Finance) Act 1973; Channel Tunnel Bill 1974.
[9] 864 H.C. Deb., col. 479 *et seq.*, Written Answers (November 22, 1973) and see Friedmann & Garner (eds.), 'Government Enterprise', Chap. III, p.70,n.71 (Daintith), and Friedmann (ed.), 'Public and Private Enterprise in Mixed Economies', Chap. V, pp.212, 218,n.92 (Daintith).
[10] H.C. 314 (1967-8), para. 76 *et seq.*
[11] *Ibid.*, Q.2973.

or partly financed out of public funds will be discussed below[12] but the desirability of specific statutory authority for such an arrangement is just as relevant to the acquisition of undertakings such as Rolls-Royce Ltd. and Beagle or the acquisition of shares in Cammell Laird. Certainly the Rolls-Royce (Purchase) Act 1971 did not contain provisions about Parliamentary control but express statutory authority for investing public money in such undertakings does at least bring the problem to the attention of the House more specifically than inclusion in the Estimates alone. This can, however, be done by other means as will be discussed below and it is arguable whether statute is so much more effective than other means of drawing a matter to the attention of the House.

Specific legislation may still be necessary even where Ministers have wide discretionary powers to provide assistance because the sums involved are too large relative to the total amount available. This was the position with regard to British Leyland Ltd. The company was provided with interim assistance up to £100 million in the form of guarantees by two House of Commons resolutions under s.8(8) of the Industry Act 1972.[13] But the British Leyland Act 1975 empowers the expenditure of up to £265 million for the acquisition of shares in the company whereas further assistance after 1976 will be made available under the Industry Acts 1972 and 1975.[14] The British Leyland Act enabled the Government to go outside the limits of s.8 of the 1972 Act both financially[15] and otherwise[16] before its amendment by the Industry Act 1975 and also prevented too great a pre-emption of resources available under these Acts at least for the time being.[17] Again, the Petroleum and Submarine Pipelines Act 1975, s.43 empowers the Secretary of State to pay the Bank of England any losses up to £350 million of the Bank in respect of loans or guarantees given to Burmah Oil Ltd. Such sums would not have been available under the Industry Act. It is also revealing that statutory authority was sought months after the guarantee had been given by the Government.[18]

---

[12] Chapter V.

[13] 883 H.C. Deb., col. 1725 (December 18, 1974) and 892 H.C. Deb., col. 1547 (May 21, 1975).

[14] *Ibid.*, col. 1429.

[15] The upper limit of expenditure under s.8 was £550 million of which £250 million had been authorised, see 886 H.C. Deb., col. 1267 (February 18, 1975).

[16] Section 8(3b) was repealed by Sch.4, Pt.I,s.2(b) to the Industry Act 1975. The Ryder Report pointed out that s.8 could not be used to buy shares from existing shareholders — H.C. 342 (1974-5), Chap. 15.24.

[17] Mr. Mikardo taunted the Government with having hypothecated for British Leyland the only money available to the National Enterprise Board and added, 'There is no National Enterprise Board, there is a British Leyland holding company which is called the National Enterprise Board': see 893 H.C. Deb., col. 1412 (June 18, 1975).

[18] The rescue operation was announced to the House on January 15, 1975 (884 H.C. Deb., col. 448).

STATUTORY INSTRUMENTS AND AFFIRMATIVE RESOLUTIONS

The next most formal method to statute for authorising financial assistance is by a statutory instrument which is subject to the approval of the House of Commons. This was the method provided for investment schemes under the Industrial Expansion Act 1968. Two aluminium smelters were authorised under these provisions.[19] The Minister who was in charge of the negotiations with the companies concerned has written that far greater control was exercised by our EFTA partners than by Parliament.[20] Debates on affirmative resolutions are subject to a time limit of one and a half hours.[21] Whilst debates on a specific statutory provision authorising expenditure may take considerably longer,[22] the length of a debate is no indication of its depth. Debates on a Bill do provide the opportunity for discussion of detailed amendments but there is little scope for this in one-clause Acts or single clauses in larger Acts which, as we saw above, are often used for this purpose.[23] It is not possible to amend a statutory instrument though it can be withdrawn by the Minister and a new instrument made. Both procedures put the burden on the Government to make time available for bringing the matter to the attention of the House which can, however, also apply to provisions which do not have the force of a statute or statutory instrument.

Under the Highlands and Islands (Shipping Services) Act 1960, s.2(3), any assistance to those providing shipping services which exceeds £10,000 must be authorised by the House of Commons by a resolution approving a draft undertaking which has been laid before it.[24]

There is a similar procedure under s.8 of the Industry Act 1972 which provides for selective financial assistance to benefit the economy as distinct from regional selective assistance under s.7. Under s.8(8), any assistance in excess of £5 million has to be authorised by a

---

[19] S.I. 1968 Nos. 1874 and 1875.

[20] DELL, 'Political Responsibility and Industry,' p.120.

[21] S.O. 3.

[22] e.g. debates in the House of Commons on the Fort William Pulp and Paper Mills Bill 1963 lasted altogether 4 hours and 20 minutes — see 675 H.C. Deb., col. 1377 *et seq.* and 677 H.C. Deb., col. 167 *et seq.* Debates in the House of Commons on the Rolls-Royce Purchase Bill 1971 lasted 12 hours — see 811 H.C. Deb., col. 814-1047 (February 11, 1971). The British Leyland Bill was debated in the House of Commons for 6½ hours *in toto,* see 892 H.C. Deb., col. 1419 (May 21, 1975) and 893 H.C. Deb., col. 1099 (June 16, 1975).

[23] In both the Rolls-Royce and the British Leyland Bills the main debates in the committee stage were on the motion that the clause stand part of the Bill.

[24] For debates on these undertakings see 651 H.C. Deb., col. 99 (December 11, 1961), 866 H.C. Deb., col. 362 (December 11, 1973), 872 H.C. Deb., col. 375 (April 9, 1974) and see Friedmann & Garner, *op. cit.,* p.73 and 897 H.C. Deb., col. 433 (August 5, 1975).

resolution of the House of Commons except in cases of urgency[25] when a statement concerning the assistance has to be laid before each House. As we have seen,[26] this provision was used on two occasions to authorise interim assistance to British Leyland.[27] It was also used to provide assistance to Norton Villiers Triumph Ltd.[28] The assistance was in the form of export guarantees and it was the first time that the Industry Act had been used for this purpose instead of the Export Guarantees Act 1968.[29] This led to a storm of protest by the Opposition who could not obtain confirmation from the Secretary of State that the company had been refused export cover by the Export Credits Guarantee Department,[30] although this was confirmed in a later debate by the Under-Secretary of State.[31] The Opposition, therefore, accused the Government wrongly, as it turned out, of acting against the letter of the Act by providing assistance even though it could be appropriately provided by other means[32] and of "blackmail" by withholding assistance under the Act until the company entered into an agreement with the newly formed workers' co-operative at Meriden to sell their motor-bikes.[33]

The assistance given to the Meriden co-operative under s.8 is a good example of not using the affirmative resolution procedure in s.8(8) because the sum granted fell just short of £5 million, i.e. £4.95 million.[34] Even nearer the limit was the guarantee of £5 million to Alfred Herbert Ltd. which was provided without an affirmative resolution.[35]

Each Government has been equally guilty of such fine calculations. The Conservative Government provided Norton Villiers Triumph Ltd. with £4.872 million of assistance which as Mr. Biffen acidly

---

[25] 'Where the Secretary of State is satisfied that the payment or undertaking is urgently needed at a time when it is impracticable to obtain the approval of the Commons House of Parliament.' This was used in the case of assistance to Kearney & Trecker Marwin Ltd. — H.C. 619 (1975-6), para. 57(f).

[26] *Supra*, n.13.

[27] On the first occasion the debate lasted two and a half hours and on the second occasion, which took place immediately after the second reading of the British Leyland Bill, one and a half hours.

[28] 887 H.C. Deb., col. 1670 (March 5, 1975). The debate lasted three hours.

[29] Amended in 1970 and 1975.

[30] *Ibid.*, col. 1675.

[31] Industry Bill, Standing Committee E, col. 620 *et seq.* (April 8, 1975).

[32] Section 8(1c).

[33] 887 H.C. Deb., col. 1684. The atmosphere of the debate was not helped, either, by some of the dictatorial language used by Ministers, *ibid.*, cols. 1707 and 1727.

[34] 878 H.C. Deb., col. 13, Written Answers (July 29, 1974). The Opposition twice raised this matter in the House because they feared that further aid would be provided without Parliamentary approval, see 878 H.C. Deb., cols. 481 and 495 (July 30, 1974).

[35] 893 H.C. Deb., col. 310, Written Answers (June 16, 1975). The guarantee was raised to £15 million by affirmative resolution on July 9, 1975, 895 H.C. Deb., col. 671.

observed fell tantalisingly short of the figure which would require Commons' approval.[36]

The affirmative resolution procedure under s.8(8) of the Industry Act 1972 was also avoided in the case of International Computers Ltd. when assistance was made available under the Science and Technology Act 1965 instead of the Industry Act as was originally intended by the Government.[37] The Minister assured the House that the change was made for administrative reasons. 'The reason is that we believe it will be more convenient to continue to give assistance for research and development under the Act [Science and Technology Act] and that as the general principle we should confine the Bill [Industry Bill] to those areas in which we do not already have powers.'[38] It is probable that the need for Parliamentary approval under s.8 played no part in the change of mind as this provision was only added to the Bill as a result of pressure by M.Ps. after this explanation was given to the House,[39] but, as Mr. Biffen pointed out, the Commons were thereby deprived of the opportunity for a debate.[40] The whole history of assistance to I.C.L. provides an interesting illustration of the extent to which Parliamentary control varies in accordance with the legislation under which assistance is provided.

Assistance was first provided on the creation of I.C.L. as a result of a merger and was embodied in the Computer Merger Scheme 1968 made under the Industrial Expansion Act 1968.[41] Like the Aluminium Smelter schemes this was a Statutory Instrument subject to Parliamentary approval and was debated accordingly.[42] The first £14 million instalment of a new package of £40 million assistance which was eventually provided under the Science and Technology Act 1965 was announced in a 130-word statement which led to four columns of questions.[43] The second instalment was announced in the House a year later at rather greater length and led to about the same number of questions.[44] Assistance is also provided to I.C.L. by the Government's purchasing policy of computers for Government use. Large computers are acquired from I.C.L. by single-tender procedures subject to satis-

---

[36] 853 H.C. Deb., col. 40 (March 19, 1973).
[37] 840 H.C. Deb., col. 34 *et seq.* (July 3, 1972).
[38] 841 H.C. Deb., col. 2331 (July 28, 1972), Report Stage of Industry Bill.
[39] A new clause requiring Commons approval for expenditure in excess of £1 million was defeated later on July 28, 1972 (841 H.C. Deb., col. 2386 *et seq.*) and the provision which is now in the Act was moved by the Minister on July 31, 1972 (842 H.C. Deb., col. 254).
[40] 859 H.C. Deb., col. 534 (July 4, 1973).
[41] S.I. 1968 No. 990.
[42] 766 H.C. Deb., col. 1495 (June 21, 1968). The merger was first announced in the House of Commons in a statement on March 21, 1968 (761 H.C. Deb., col. 607).
[43] 840 H.C. Deb., col. 34 *et seq.* (July 3, 1972).
[44] 859 H.C. Deb., col. 529 (July 4, 1973).

factory price, performance and delivery dates. This policy, which slightly changed the previous practice described in a memorandum to the Select Committee on Science & Technology,[45] was announced in a Written Answer.[46]

CIVIL AVIATION ACT

Contract is also the medium under which assistance is given to the aircraft industry under the Civil Aviation Act 1949. Assistance is given in the form of launching aid[47] which is an interest-free contribution to the launching costs of the aircraft or engine repayable as a levy on sales. A recent example of this was the proposed investment by the Government of £40 million in Hawker-Siddeley's HS. 146 airliner. This was announced by the Minister at a press conference on August 30, 1973 when Parliament was not sitting.[48] The details were published in Hansard in answer to a Question on October 22, 1973.[49] The abandonment of the project was announced to the House on December 9, 1974[50] and was followed by an adjournment debate.[51]

Assistance to Rolls-Royce for the RB211 engine and for the development as distinct from the production of Concorde was similarly provided under the Civil Aviation Act. It is very interesting to look with hindsight at how these projects were presented to Parliament. The American order obtained by Rolls-Royce was announced to the House in a brief statement by Mr. Benn amidst a shower of congratulations.[52] He could not give figures for the Government's launching aid but said that 70 per cent of the cost of the project was being discussed. The normal figure for launching aid is 50 per cent. Later, he announced in a Written Answer that the maximum figure of aid for this 'very promising project' was £47 million.[53] This was the way in which Parliament was committed to a project which later escalated to several times the original estimate.[54]

---

[45] H.C. 137 (1969-70), p.442.
[46] 812 H.C. Deb., col. 419, Written Answers (March 2, 1971).
[47] This is described in Cmnd. 4860 (Annex A) — the White Paper on Rolls-Royce. Launching aid for civil aircraft will not be available to British Aerospace after nationalisation (Aircraft and Shipbuilding Industries Bill, cl. 46) but assistance may be provided up to £50 million under cl. 45.
[48] *The Guardian,* August 30, 1973 and see *Flight International,* September 6, 1973.
[49] 861 H.C. Deb., col. 687.
[50] 883 H.C. Deb., col. 45.
[51] 883 H.C. Deb., col. 970 (December 12, 1974).
[52] 762 H.C. Deb., col. 44 (April 1, 1968).
[53] 788 H.C. Deb., col. 279, Written Answers (October 22, 1969).
[54] Launching aid of over £40 million for the more powerful version of the RB211 engine was announced in Written Answers, see 882 H.C. Deb., col. 621 (December 5, 1974) and 893 H.C. Deb., col. 539 (June 20, 1975) and see *Trade & Industry,* June 27, 1975 and 897 H.C. Deb., col. 233, Written Answers (August 6, 1975).

The prime example of escalation is of course Concorde. The fateful statement that an agreement had been signed with France to build a supersonic airliner was made to the House on November 29, 1962.[55] The estimated cost to Britain was put at £75-85 million! In the brief debate[56] that followed anxiety was expressed by some M.Ps. Mr. Grimond asked for a debate and another M.P. requested a White Paper but was told that commercial secrets were involved. Mr. Rankin threatened to raise the matter on the adjournment of the House which he did in the following month.[57] Thus it was left to a backbencher to instigate a debate on a project which the Select Committee on Estimates characterised as an 'example of executive action which commits Parliament to an unspecified heavy expenditure . . . on which returns must be problematical.'[58]

INDUSTRY ACT 1972

Except in the case of assistance over £5 million under s.8, which has been discussed above, there is no legal obligation to obtain Parliamentary approval for assistance. On the contrary, one of the subjects about which successive Governments have refused to answer Questions are the details of financial assistance to individual companies.[59] This must now be considerably qualified. Assistance given to individual firms under the Industry Act 1972, where it is of great and immediate public interest, is normally announced as soon as possible. The Government has made statements to Parliament about large-scale grants such as Cammell Laird,[60] Govan Shipbuilders Ltd.,[61] Court Line,[62] Burmah Oil,[63] Ferranti Ltd.[64] and Chrysler UK Ltd.[65] In other cases the information has been provided in answer to Parliamentary Questions, e.g. Alfred Herbert Ltd.,[66] Bear Brand Ltd.,[67] The Meriden Workers' Co-operative,[68] The Scottish News Enterprises Ltd.[69] and

[55] 668 H.C. Deb., col. 670.
[56] Seven columns.
[57] 669 H.C. Deb., col. 1627 (December 21, 1962).
[58] H.C. 42 (1963-4), para. 89.
[59] H.C. 393 (1971-2), App. 9 and H.C. 347 (1971-2), Vol. II, Qs.131-3.
[60] 835 H.C. Deb., col. 1282 (April 25, 1972).
[61] 832 H.C. Deb., col. 49 (February 28, 1972).
[62] 875 H.C. Deb., col. 1556 (June 26, 1974).
[63] 884 H.C. Deb., col. 448 (January 15, 1975).
[64] 892 H.C. Deb., col. 457 (May 14, 1975).
[65] 902 H.C. Deb., col. 1164 (December 16, 1975).
[66] 880 H.C. Deb., col. 33, Written Answers (November 4, 1974); 893 H.C. Deb. col. 310, Written Answers (June 16, 1975).
[67] 889 H.C. Deb., col. 1218, Written Answers (March 27, 1975).
[68] 878 H.C. Deb., col. 13 *et seq.*, Written Answers (July 29, 1974).
[69] 878 H.C. Deb., col. 369, Written Answers (July 31, 1974). Details were given in reply to a debate on the date for the Adjournment, 878 H.C. Deb., col. 108 (July 29, 1974).

Kirkby Manufacturing & Engineering Co. Ltd.[70] In all these cases the information supplied in answer to Questions had already been publicly announced.[71] In the last case Mr. Benn, when giving the information, stressed that information about past assistance was only given exceptionally and with the consent of the parties concerned. On an earlier occasion the Department said in evidence to the Expenditure Committee that where regional aid was of general interest agreement was sought to make it public.[72] It is difficult to believe, however, that Mr. Benn obtained the consent of the twenty leading firms whose total receipts from grants he made public in July and September 1974[73] to show the extent to which private industry was subsidised. He has also announced that payments to establishments of regional development grant exceeding £25,000 and payments to companies or individuals to whom regional selective assistance amounting to £10,000 of loan is offered from July 31, 1974 will be published quarterly.[74]

Although these arrangements go considerably beyond the previous practice of publishing global sums in the Annual Report under the Industry Act where only a few large grants were mentioned by name, the vast majority of grants are still confidential. This confidentiality was strongly defended by Ministers.[75] The agreements with companies giving them selective assistance are also regarded as confidential to the Department.[76] In the case of the Kirkby Workers' Co-operative the Secretary of State said that the main terms and conditions were exceptionally described in the statement laid before the House at the request of the Industrial Development Advisory Board.[77] Some of the terms were also given 'exceptionally and with consent of the company' in a Written Answer.[78] This exception is, however, becoming more the rule. The terms and conditions of the other two workers' co-operatives were also revealed to the House.[79] The conditions attaching to the

[70] 883 H.C. Deb., col. 1, Written Answers (December 9, 1974).
[71] In the case of aid for Triang Pedigree there seems to have been no announcement in Parliament, but see *Trade & Industry*, May 23, 1975, p.443. All the firms granted assistance under s.8 were named in the debate on the resolution to raise the financial limits for the aggregate amount payable under the section: 886 H.C. Deb. col. 1268 *et seq.* (February 18, 1975).
[72] H.C. 85-I (1973-4), App. 3.
[73] 878 H.C. Deb., col. 14, Written Answers (July 29, 1974) and 885 H.C. Deb., col. 351, Written Answers (January 31, 1975). For a table of grants to leading shipbuilding firms, see 881 H.C. Deb., col. 542, Written Answers (November 22, 1974).
[74] 878 H.C. Deb., col. 371, Written Answers (July 31, 1974). These arrangements have been extended to some industry-wide schemes under the Industry Act 1972, s.8.
[75] 886 H.C. Deb., cols. 954 and 1294 (February 17 and 18, 1975).
[76] H.C. 304 (1974), Q. 514 *et seq.* and 885 H.C. Deb., col. 316, Written Answers (January 30, 1975).
[77] *Ibid.*, and see Industry Act 1972, s.9(4).
[78] 886 H.C. Deb., col. 147, Written Answers (February 12, 1975).
[79] Meriden — 878 H.C. Deb., col. 15, Written Answers (July 29, 1974); Scottish News Enterprises — 878 H.C. Deb., col. 108 (July 29, 1974).

guarantee for British Leyland have again been given to the House[80] as have the arrangements for financial support to Ferranti Ltd.[81] The agreement with Chrysler has been published in the minutes of evidence of the Expenditure Committee.[82]

Though announcements of assistance under the Industry Act either through statements or Written Answers are becoming increasingly common, they are not obligatory as Ministers have not been slow at times to point out.[83] It is interesting that, under the Petroleum and Submarine Pipe-Lines Act 1975, s.42(3), the Secretary of State is under an obligation to lay before each House a statement immediately after a loan or guarantee is made under that section for the development of petroleum resources. It would be impossible to implement a similar provision in the case of assistance under the Industry Act but it would be perfectly feasible to convert the Secretary of State's announcement about quarterly publication of aid above a certain figure into a statutory obligation.

CONCLUSION

In the foregoing pages the extent to which Parliament plays a part in determining the expenditure of public money for private industry has been examined. Legally, all expenditure needs Parliamentary approval in the Appropriation Act but this is a formality as far as individual estimates are concerned as these are rarely debated and the Expenditure Committee, unlike the Estimates Committee, does not issue a separate report on Supplementary Estimates. Where specific legislation is needed to authorise assistance because existing legislation is not adequate there is the possibility of detailed discussion on the Bill though this may not necessarily be effective in practice. Similarly, where Parliamentary approval is necessary by statutory instrument or resolution there is opportunity for less detailed discussion though no possibility of amendment. But these cases are the exception rather than the rule when wide discretionary powers are vested in the Government, as is the case under the Civil Aviation Act 1949, the Science and Technology Act 1965, the Industry Act 1972 and even the Highways Act 1959.[84] When acting under these Acts the Minister is under no obli-

---

[80] 889 H.C. Deb., col. 216, Written Answers (March 27, 1975).

[81] 892 H.C. Deb., col. 457 *et seq.* (May 14, 1975).

[82] H.C. 104-i (1975-6), p.9.

[83] 853 H.C. Deb., col. 35 (March 19, 1973); 892 H.C. Deb., col. 460 (May 14, 1975).

[84] The use of this Act to provide assistance to W & C French (Construction) Ltd. to complete road contracts caused concern to the Public Accounts Committee because it enables unlimited payments to be made without prior Parliamentary approval, though in this case Parliament was informed retrospectively — H.C. 584 (1975-6), para. 45 *et seq.*

gation to inform the Commons about the granting of assistance though statements are now usually made where large sums are at stake. But such statements provide little scope for debate and in any case the matter is by then a fait accompli. This was particularly marked in cases like Rolls-Royce and Concorde where huge sums of money many times the original estimates were thereby committed for the future.

Parliament is at the moment gravely deficient in scrutinising expenditure before the money is committed. There should be in the case of major items of expenditure such as Rolls-Royce and Concorde a White Paper setting out the proposals before money is committed by the Government[85] which should be debated. There was a Green Paper and a White Paper on the proposed Channel Tunnel which were debated but this was one of the exceptional cases which needed legislation.[86] Similarly an abridged version of the Ryder Report on British Leyland which the Government accepted as the basis for assistance was published.[87]

For detailed scrutiny a Select Committee is needed. A Select Committee cannot function effectively in the middle of a crisis. The Trade and Industry Sub-Committee of the Expenditure Committee discovered this when they were hearing evidence just after the collapse of Rolls-Royce. The Deputy Secretary of the Department of Trade and Industry asked to be excused from answering questions on this issue because of the delicate negotiations which were going on. The Committee after deliberating on the matter decided not to press him further at that point but came back to the case later in their inquiry when negotiations were complete.[88] Similarly, their examination of the Secretary of State on the rescue of Upper Clyde Shipbuilders Ltd. was made after he had announced the terms of the rescue operation in the House of Commons and was more of a post mortem than a probing into the future.[89] This perhaps excessive caution seems now to have been thrown to the winds as the Trade and Industry Sub-committee examining the motor car industry questioned Lord Stokes of British Leyland

---

[85] The Expenditure Committee's report on 'Public Money in the Private Sector' recommended an annual White Paper in such cases, see H.C. 347 (1971-2), para. 277. They also welcomed publication of the White Paper on Rolls-Royce (Cmnd. 4860) and the Hill, Samuel Report on Upper Clyde Shipbuilders (Cmnd. 4918).

[86] 857 H.C. Deb., col. 1867 (June 15, 1973); 861 H.C. Deb., col. 1494 (October 25, 1973).

[87] H.C. 342 (1974-5) and 890 H.C. Deb., col. 1742 (April 24, 1975).

[88] H.C. 347 (1971-2), para. 57.

[89] *Ibid.*, vol. III, Minutes of Evidence p.671 *et seq.* This also happened when Mr. Benn was examined by the Scottish Affairs Committee after an earlier rescue operation of U.C.S., see H.C.397 (1968-9), p.249.

about its application for Government aid whilst it was being investigated by Lord Ryder on behalf of the Government.[90] The Committee also examined the Secretary of State for Industry about Aston Martin's application whilst negotiations with that firm were still continuing.[91] In neither case did the Committee report before the issue was settled.

The Select Committee on Expenditure recommended in 1972 that a Select Committee should be appointed 'at the time when a substantial sum of public money is committed. We believe that a Select Committee on Concorde appointed in 1962 or on the RB211 appointed in 1968 could have had a useful continuing function; and that in the event of a major commitment to V/S.T.O.L., the next generation of aircraft engines or a 'stretched' version of Concorde, to take three possible examples, a Select Committee should be appointed.'[92] They thought that such a committee should be located under the umbrella of the Expenditure Committee.

Other suggestions for a Select Committee on a specific project have been made. In the case of the Channel Tunnel a new clause which would have established a Select Committee before £20 million had been spent was rejected on the Report Stage of the Channel Tunnel (Initial Finance) Bill 1973.[93] Significantly after the General Election, the Labour Government, when reintroducing the Channel Tunnel Bill, announced that a small high-powered group of independent advisers would be appointed to review all financial and economic assessments of the project.[94] The project was abandoned before the review was completed but it is revealing that a Select Committee was not entrusted with the review.

When cancellation of the H.S. 146 airliner was under discussion, there was also a suggestion for the appointment of a Select Committee[95] and Mr. Benn, when announcing the cancellation to the House, said that he was considering how the Commons could be provided with fuller opportunities for discussing this type of project in future.[96]

The Select Committee on Science and Technology in their Report on the prospects of the United Kingdom computer industry in the 1970's[97] made recommendations which were highly relevant to the £40

---

[90] H.C. 617-I (1974-5), Q. 298 *et seq.*
[91] H.C. 617-I (1974-5), Q. 569 *et seq.*
[92] H.C. 347 (1971-2), para. 276.
[93] 864 H.C. Deb., col. 203 (November 8, 1973). A similar clause was rejected on the Report Stage of the Concorde Aircraft Bill 1973, see 850 H.C. Deb., col. 1495 (February 15, 1973).
[94] 872 H.C. Deb., col. 961 (April 30, 1974).
[95] 881 H.C. Deb., col. 594 (November 14, 1974).
[96] 883 H.C. Deb., col. 46 (December 9, 1974).
[97] H.C. 621 (1970-1).

million package of assistance given to I.C.L. in 1972 and 1973[98] but in their follow-up report they criticised the Government for not implementing their recommendations as to the way in which the increased aid should be provided.[99] In particular, they pointed out the dangers of concentrating aid on one firm.[100]

The same committee had more success with their investigation of the choice of a nuclear reactor for the next stage of Britain's nuclear programme. The energy resources sub-committee of the Science and Technology Committee heard evidence on the matter for three successive sessions. It reopened the issue when a Government decision seemed imminent and heard evidence from the Chief Inspector of Nuclear Installations as well as the nuclear construction industry and the Central Electricity Generating Board.[101] It firmly recommended that the evidence publicly available was not sufficient to warrant buying American reactors. The chairman felt strongly that, where millions of pounds were at stake, the citizen had a right to ask questions through his elected representatives and that this was not a matter to be left to experts, especially when they disagreed. After a debate on the issue,[102] the Government eventually accepted the Committee's recommendation in favour of a British nuclear reactor.[103]

This is a good example of how a Select Committee can investigate even a complex technical issue in depth and make recommendations before the Government has made a decision committing large sums of public money on a major new technological development. There is no inherent reason why this should not be possible in other cases of this nature of which the Expenditure Committee gave some examples. Whether the committee should be a sub-committee of an existing Select Committee or be appointed as an ad hoc committee would depend on the subject-matter. As we have seen, it may be more difficult to utilise a Select Committee in the case of an urgent rescue operation but even here the Trade and Industry Sub-Committee has broken new ground in its investigation of the motor car industry though it did not report in time to influence the Government's decisions. Due to the speed of the Chrysler rescue operation, the Sub-Committee's investigation in that case was inevitably *ex post facto*. The crucial factor which determined the Committee to undertake the investigation was the cavalier treatment of the House of Commons by the Government which the Committee felt had precluded the House from usefully examining

---

[98] v. supra, nn. 43 and 44.
[99] H.C. 309 (1972-3).
[100] *Ibid.*, para. 56.
[101] H.C. 145 (1973-4).
[102] 872 H.C. Deb., col. 1344 (May 2, 1974).
[103] 876 H.C. Deb., col. 1357 (July 10, 1974).

or discussing the rescue deal. The matters which particularly disturbed the Committee were first, that the report of the Central Policy Review Staff, who had been requested to review the motor vehicle industry, was not published until the day that the Chrysler rescue was announced, though it had been in the Government's hands for weeks.[104] Secondly, the Committee was disgusted with the Government's reply to its own report on the motor vehicle industry which the Committee felt had not been read properly let alone answered after five months' study by the Departments. Finally, the Committee deprecated that the debate on the motion to approve the rescue deal took place thirty-one hours after its announcement and lasted one and a half hours. The Committee thought that the House was being used as a rubber stamp by the Government and one of the purposes of its investigation was, 'to provide the House with the information the Government should have given it, and to discover whether the Government's actions warranted suspicion, or whether they were simply the result of thoughtless discourtesy.'[105]

The Committee's report may, therefore, be seen as a real assertion of Parliamentary scrutiny, though of necessity after the event. If the Government responds to this searing attack and heeds the advice of the Committee to make more information available in good time before the debate, a more meaningful discussion will be possible,[106] even though the vote, where this is necessary, is unlikely to be affected. Barring accidents,[107] or a backbench revolt, this is the most that the House as a whole can normally hope to achieve under our present political system once the Government has made its decision. Only by using Select Committees where possible to investigate before public money is committed can the House hope to strengthen its influence over public expenditure in this field.

---

[104] H.C. 596-I (1975-6) para. 27 seq.
[105] *Ibid.*, para. 35.
[106] For similar criticism of inadequate information on the motion for approval of the Alfred Herbert Ltd. rescue, see 901 H.C. Deb., col. 1624 (December 2, 1975).
[107] As happened in the debate to reduce the Secretary of State's salary on February 11, 1976, 905 H.C. Deb., col. 461.

CHAPTER TWO

PROVISION OF AID BY GOVERNMENT DEPARTMENTS

HAVING examined the role of Parliament in the provision of aid to private industry we must now look at the decision-making process of Government Departments from the point of view of both the internal machinery and the extent to which the Departments draw on external advice. As we shall see, the internal and external machinery is geared to expert evaluation of the project before public money is committed. It does not provide a public forum where the issues can be debated. Select Committees could and to a limited extent already do provide such a forum.

THE CHANNEL TUNNEL

Another mechanism which could be utilised for this purpose is the public inquiry. There was a call for such an inquiry when the proposal for a Channel Tunnel was under discussion but both the Conservative and later the Labour Government resisted such a proposal.[1] In view of the experience with the Roskill Commission which took two and a half years to report on the siting of the Third London Airport this is not surprising. However, in the case of the Channel Tunnel there was no formal machinery for consulting the public though there were public meetings at which the proposals were discussed as well as consultation with local authorities.[2]

After the General Election, the Labour Government set up an independent inquiry of high powered experts to review the project. The report was not received until after the project had been abandoned and it was then published.[3] This was an expert inquiry into the economic and financial studies which had already been undertaken. The committee concentrated on the economic and financial issues rather than environmental factors on which they had no special expertise. The committee made some criticisms of the studies, in particular of the

---

[1] 863 H.C. Deb., col. 1241 (November 8, 1973), 872 H.C. Deb. col. 1036 (April 30, 1974).
[2] Cmnd 5430, para. 8:11.
[3] The Channel Tunnel and Alternative Cross Channel Services (HMSO); 1975.

appointment by the Government of the same consultants as the Channel Companies. They also criticised these consultants' studies for not including sufficient examination of alternatives. But their main complaint was that they were appointed at the end of the story rather than the beginning.[4] They were asked about how a decision should be taken after it had been reached and when the studies were too advanced to be influenced by any advice.

This led the committee to consider the wider question of the role of such a body if it had been appointed earlier. They felt that an expert group had a limited function to perform in the case of a major project of this nature. They said that, 'An expert group may clear the ground but will not always carry conviction on the matters in dispute. The public would also be in a better position to evaluate the arguments if as much as possible were published in an accessible form.'[5] They thought that a body similar to the Royal Commission on Environmental Pollution or the Monopolies Commission might provide a solution for investigating such major projects. It would have expertise and the independence necessary to canvass public opinion and advise on interdepartmental issues.[6] Such a body would provide a forum for public examination of the issues which was so obviously lacking in the case of the Channel Tunnel.

CONCORDE

Though the committee only concerned itself with the economic and financial studies, the Government also carried out studies on safety and noise and commissioned Economic Consultants Ltd. to carry out a study on the economic and social impact of the tunnel on Kent. This was a much wider range of studies than preceded the decision to build Concorde. In the case of Concorde a technical committee was set up in 1956 consisting of representatives of the Ministries concerned, the aircraft manufacturers, aero-engine firms and the Air Corporations to study the feasibility of a supersonic aircraft.[7] £700,000 was spent on research studies. The committee reported in 1959 that serious design work should be undertaken and feasibility study contracts worth £300,000 were placed with the main groups of manufacturers. The manufacturers were asked to consider foreign collaboration and BAC's project was regarded as the most promising in 1960. These were

---

[4] *Ibid.*, Chap. 5.1.
[5] *Ibid.*, Chap. 5.4.8.
[6] *Ibid.*, Chap. 5.4.9.
[7] For history of the project, see H.C. 42 (1963-4), Second Report from Estimates Committee, para. 70 *et seq.*

briefly the events leading up to the Anglo-French Treaty of 1962. The lack of Treasury participation in the discussions leading up to the signing of the Treaty and the supervision of the project thereafter was severely criticised by the Estimates Committee as was the lack of attention paid to the financial in contrast to the technical considerations.[8] What is even more marked in contrast to the Third London Airport and even the Channel Tunnel is the complete lack of public participation. Concorde will not of course have the same physical impact as either of the other two projects would have had but noise would not have been the only issue of wide public interest. There were also questions like radiation, employment prospects and the policy of investing huge sums in supersonic air travel which would have merited public discussion. It is a mark of the progress that has been made in the years that have elapsed since Concorde to contrast the narrow technical studies made in that case with the very much broader issues investigated in connection with the Channel Tunnel. What was lacking in both instances was a public forum where these issues could be probed in depth before the decision was made.

RB211

When one turns from Concorde to a project like the RB 211 engine the case for public discussion of the issues may seem weaker. The initiative here quite clearly came from the private firm of Rolls-Royce who felt that they must break through into this new generation of engines in order to remain in the big league. This is not dissimilar to the feeling in 1956 that we must go in for supersonic aircraft to remain in the league-table of major aircraft manufacturers. But whereas the initiative in 1956 came from the Government, the Lockheed contract for the RB 211 engine was regarded as primarily the responsibility of Rolls-Royce. This had very important consequences. Though the Government made its own technical studies to test the commercial viability of the project before it committed itself to a higher than normal percentage of launching aid, nevertheless it was later admitted by Mr. Benn, the Minister concerned, that he took the view that it was basically a commercial venture and he relied to a considerable extent on the expertise and prestige of Rolls-Royce.[9] Because the firm was putting its entire resources at stake it was felt that it was not necessary to assess every detail. We have been told that this particular lesson has been

---

[8] *Ibid.,* para. 84.
[9] Report of Inspectors holding investigation under the Companies Act, paras. 267 & 8 (H.M.S.O.), 1973.

learnt.[10] But Mr. Benn also admitted that the Government did not have the expertise to check the figures of the most experienced air engine company in Britain.[11] This has also changed.

Since the Rolls-Royce contract in 1962 there has been a reorganisation of the responsibilities for civil aircraft projects.[12] The Procurement Executive located in the Ministry of Defence is now responsible for giving technical advice on the project and on the contract to the Department of Industry which is responsible for the policy of the project. The Procurement Executive has specialist contract, accounting and scientific and engineering services. It was because 'procurement is a specialised function which can only be carried out efficiently by people with specialised skills' that the Rayner Report[13] in 1971 recommended the creation of the Procurement Executive, which is responsible for all defence procurement as well as technical advice in civil aircraft projects.

SELECTIVE ASSISTANCE UNDER THE INDUSTRY ACT 1972

When the negotiations in relation to the setting up of aluminium smelters were being conducted there was no specialised unit within the relevant Government Department for this purpose. An ad hoc multi-disciplinary inter-departmental team of officials was specially set up.[14] The Chairman of Rio-Tinto Zinc Ltd., which was one of the firms involved, paid a glowing tribute to the civil servants, though he added that, 'it would be better if Government used public servants who were doing nothing but that particular operation while it is on, instead of trying to deal with so many other things, because it is particularly complex.'[15] Though nothing came of the proposal to have a post mortem about the negotiations to see what lessons could be learnt about how to handle such matters, there was a complete reorganisation of the Department of Trade and Industry to administer the Industry Act 1972. There were some changes when the Departments of Industry and Trade were separated in 1974 but the basic framework of the reorganisation designed to inject industrial and commercial expertise into the Department remained intact.

---

[10] H.C. 347-II (1971-2), Q.2486, and see this point emphasised in connection with the H.S.146 project — *Flight International,* September 6, 1973, p.395. Nationalisation of the aircraft industry will virtually eliminate the problem.

[11] 811 H.C. Deb., col.66 (February 8, 1971).

[12] See H.C. 347-II (1971-2), p.605 *et seq.*

[13] Cmnd. 4641 (1971), para. 3.

[14] See DELL *op cit.,* p. 116 *et seq.*

[15] H.C. 347-I (1971-2), Q. 1370.

Apart from the Permanent Secretary there is a Second Permanent Secretary and under them are several Deputy Secretaries, one of whom is Director of the Industrial Development Unit,[16] recruited from outside the Department. He has a staff who come from the City, industry and Government. In the regions where there are substantial assisted areas[17] namely Scotland, Wales,[18] Northern, Yorkshire and Humberside, North West and South West Regions there has also been an injection of industrial expertise by the appointment of a Regional Industrial Director recruited from the private sector on a short-term contract[19] alongside the Regional Director at Under-Secretary level.

AID UNDER SECTION 7

These regional offices[20] have delegated responsibility to deal with applications for regional selective assistance under s.7 of the Industry Act[21] up to £2 million for loans and interest relief grants on notional loans up to the same figure[22] provided that they fall within the guidelines which have been laid down for such projects and published.[23] The application is dealt with initially by the regional industrial director and his staff who see their role as helping applicants with their applications rather than as 'yes' or 'no' people.[24] They then make a report and recommendation prior to a joint decision being reached with the regional director after discussion with the Regional Industrial Development Board.[25] In the case of disagreement between the two directors the application would have to be referred to Headquarters but this has not so far happened. All applications are communicated to Headquarters so that the Department knows the overall picture of expenditure under s.7 which has to keep within the estimates agreed with the Treasury.[26]

---

[16] *Trade & Industry,* December 3, 1976.

[17] I.e., Special Development, Development and Intermediate areas.

[18] Responsibility for regional selective assistance under s.7 of the Industry Act 1972 was transferred to the Secretaries of State for Scotland and Wales from July 1, 1975: see 883 H.C. Deb., col. 712, Written Answers (December 20, 1974).

[19] H.C. 303 (1974), Q.111,p.18.

[20] The South West region has lower limits of delegated responsibility.

[21] For non-selective assistance, see below,Chap.III.

[22] H.C. 617-I (1974-5), p.4, para. 10, and 914 H.C. Deb., col. 547, Written Answers, (July 7, 1976).

[23] See Appendix D, Annual Report 1974-5, Industry Act 1972, H.C. 620 (1974-5). For revised criteria for assistance to industry, see H.C. 104-ii (1975-6) p.113 *et seq.*

[24] H.C. 327 (1972-3), Q.604, and H.C. 303 (1974), Q. 168-9, p.30.

[25] These are non-statutory bodies consisting of members drawn from industry, banking, accounting and trade unions. In Scotland and Wales they have been given a statutory basis: see Scottish Development Agency Act 1975, s.20, and Welsh Development Agency Act 1975, s.13.

[26] H.C. 617-I (1974-5), Q.17-19.

All cases outside the delegated powers, i.e. above the monetary limits or outside the guidelines, go to Headquarters where the Department has available the expertise of the Industrial Development Unit. Such cases are also referred for advice to the Industrial Development Advisory Board[27] and then to the Minister.[28] The Treasury must be informed in advance of a loan above £2 million being made within the guidelines and their approval is necessary for assistance above that figure outside the guidelines.[29] The Regional Office will make a report on applications falling outside their delegated powers.[30]

The guidelines under which selective assistance is provided under s.7 of the Industry Act 1972 divide projects into two categories. In Category A are those projects which create additional employment and for which loans at concessionary rates, interest relief grants for money obtained elsewhere and removal grants are available. Under Category B fall projects which maintain or safeguard existing employment for which loans at commercial rates are normally given only where assistance cannot be obtained from commercial sources. As much as 70 per cent of the assistance under s.7 is in the form of interest relief grant which merely involves the Department in paying the subsidy element in a loan without lending the principal.[31]

In order to fall within Category A a benefit to employment must be shown.[32] The Government apply a confidential cost-per-job yardstick to the public sector contribution figure which represents a maximum figure for the loan.[33] There is also a limit to the total amount of assistance coming from any source of public funds, which is roughly half.[34] The other criterion for aid is viability. Unless the application is for a small interest relief grant or by a firm of national standing for an interest relief grant, there will be an accountancy investigation into the audited accounts for the past three years and trading forecasts as well as an investigation into the market for the product, production facilities and management.[35] The applicant will not necessarily get the maximum amount permissible for his requirements but the sum will be

[27] Set up under s.9 of the Industry Act 1972 and consisting of members from industry, banking, accounting and trade unions.
[28] H.C. 303 (1974), Q.138, p.25.
[29] *Ibid.*, App.I, paras. 16 & 17.
[30] *Ibid.*
[31] H.C. 374 (1974-5), Q.470, and H.C. 617-I (1974-5), Q.17.
[32] Except in the case of assistance for shipyard modernisation schemes; 860 H.C. Deb., col.1157 (July 23, 1973).
[33] H.C. 303 (1974), Q.100, p.17, and Q.160, p.30 *et seq.*
[34] *Ibid.*, Q.100, and H.C. 374 (1974-5), Q.508.
[35] H.C. 303 (1974), Q.98, p.16, and see Q.136, p.24 — Regional Directors have been told that they may accept a slightly higher degree of risk than a bank manager. See also 'Criteria for Assistance to Industry' — H.C. 104-ii (1975-6), p.113, para.15.

tailored to the project's profitability, costs and the financial resources it requires.[36] The Public Accounts Committee, however, felt that the applicant's real need should be taken into account more in future.[37] An application is also not rejected because the firm was going to move into an assisted area in any case.[38]

The vast majority of cases fall within the guidelines and are viable employment creating projects.[39] But it is the small minority of rescue cases which fall outside the guidelines which have caused great difficulties and created much controversy. These cases will always be dealt with at Headquarters with the help of the Industrial Development Unit and will almost always be submitted to the Industrial Development Advisory Board and then go to the Minister and further to a Cabinet Committee in the important cases.[40]

Projects may fall outside the guidelines either because the conditions have not been satisfied or because of the type of help provided. Though the guidelines were amended by the Labour Government to enable assistance to be provided in the form of share capital,[41] guarantees or grants are still outside the normal guidelines. As regards cases falling outside the specified conditions a new category has evolved of exceptional cases to maintain employment where there is a risk of redundancies in an assisted area, taking into account the number and nature of the jobs as well as the possibilities of alternative employment.[42] Firms may be given loans on concessionary terms or interest relief grants[43] provided that the company has sound prospects of viability. It is the cases where this condition cannot be satisfied which have given rise to the greatest controversy.

Due to the deteriorating economic situation there have been an increasing number of applications from firms to be rescued. The Government have responded by waiving the condition about a contribution from outside the public sector and regarding viability as no longer a vital consideration.[44] But the Department in their evidence to the Expenditure Committee inquiry into the motor industry were adamant that they were not providing money to firms who would become

---

[36] HC 303 (1974), Q.100, p.17, and H.C. 374 (1974-5), para.53.

[37] *Ibid.*, para. 59.

[38] *Ibid.*, Q.520.

[39] *Ibid.*, Q.476 *et seq.* and App.IV. There were over 1600 Category A projects up to December 1974 compared with 26 rescue cases. See also H.C. 104-ii (1975-6), p.118, para.32.

[40] H.C. 374 (1974-5), Q.502.

[41] 872 H.C. Deb., col. 347-8, Written Answers (April 29, 1974).

[42] See Annual Report 1972-3, Industry Act 1972, H.C. 429 (1972-3), para.14, and Annual Report 1973-4, H.C. 339 (1973-4), para.21.

[43] These would normally be Category B cases.

[44] H.C. 374 (1974-5), Q.460-5 and 503, H.C. 617-I (1974-5), Q.58, H.C. 104-ii (1975-6), p.116, para.21.

permanent pensioners.[45] The Committee's Report pinpointed the underlying paradox in this evidence, 'We fail to see how a firm will avoid becoming a 'permanent pensioner' if it is not viable and is unable to make profits, and we wish to see a resolution of this apparent conflict in the Department's approach to selective assistance.'[46]

AID UNDER SECTION 8

Rescue applications arise not only under s.7 of the Industry Act 1972 but also under s.8. This section, unlike s.7, is not restricted to the assisted areas but enables assistance to be given where it is likely to benefit the economy and is in the national interest. These cases are always dealt with at Headquarters with the help of the Industrial Development Unit. All s.8 cases involving loans above £500,000, acquisition of share capital over £250,000 or grants, other than interest relief grants or removal grants, above £100,000 and any proposal for an industry-wide scheme are submitted to the Industrial Development Advisory Board.[47] Ministers have been involved in all s.8 cases[48] and the case may be considered by Ministers collectively especially if the advice of the Advisory Board is not accepted.[49]

Every s.8 case needs the approval of the Treasury. Expenditure under s.8 is not budgeted for in the Estimates in the normal way because of its unpredictability. The money is provided out of the contingency reserve — a fund which covers unforeseen expenditure by all Government Departments and which is controlled by the Treasury. Any expenditure out of this reserve has to be authorised by a Supplementary Estimate.[50] As we have seen, any project under s.8 involving expenditure over £5 million needs an affirmative resolution in the Commons and there is an overall limit of expenditure under the section of £150 million which can be raised by affirmative resolution in tranches of £100 million to £550 million.[51]

No guidelines have been laid down for the operation of s.8 so that the only criteria are those laid down in the Act. The restriction which prevented assistance being given by the Secretary of State unless it could not be provided otherwise has been repealed by the Industry Act

---

[45] H.C. 617-I (1974-5), Q.59 and 60.
[46] *Ibid.,* para. 153.
[47] H.C. 303 (1974), App.I, para.26.
[48] H.C. 617 (1974-5), para.151.
[49] H.C. 617-I (1974-5), Q.576 and 583.
[50] H.C. 617-II (1974-5), Q.2627-37, and H.C. 474 (1974-5), Q.199 *et seq.*
[51] 'Section 8 (7 & 8); s.8(5) which set December 31, 1977 as the time-limit for the operation of the section has been repealed by Sch.4, Pt.I, s.2(d), to the Industry Act 1975. The Industry (Amendment) Act 1976 increases the limit to £1600 million.

1975.[52] It meant that Aston Martin Ltd., when they originally applied for assistance, had to be referred first of all to private sources for finance.[53] A new negative factor has been added by the Government's White Paper 'Attack on Inflation'[54] which provides that the Government will interpret the national interest as including observance of the pay limit so that the Government will not give discretionary assistance under the Act to companies which have broken the pay limit. This to some extent, though by a different route, meets the criticism made by the Expenditure Committee that the containment and reduction of inflation was not mentioned by the Department in their interpretation of the national interest.[55]

The criteria laid down in s.8 of the Act which refer to the national interest and the benefit of the economy are very broad and do not lend themselves, as the Department has said, to a series of sub-criteria.[56] To interpret the national interest as meaning 'the benefit to the economy as a whole of the particular development, whether it contributes to employment, efficiency, profitability, productivity, ability to export, ability to substitute for imports, ability to provide greater social benefits to the community involved, not only in the industry but in the surrounding regions and in the country as a whole,'[57] does not give much guidance as to which of these factors will be decisive in an individual case. An attempt was, however, made by the Department to list three broad categories of cases in which assistance might be provided under s.8.[58] First, where the market mechanism does not provide support for projects which merit support on commercial grounds. Secondly, to give temporary help to a declining industry or a firm or industry in difficulties to put them back on their feet or to help a planned contraction and, thirdly to give assistance leading to wider economic or social benefits such as balance of payment considerations.

The actual assistance which has been provided under s.8 does not fall neatly into these categories. Firstly, there have been industry-wide schemes to help ageing, even if not declining, industries to modernise. The first such scheme was the Wool Textile Industry Scheme[59] which provided for capital grants for re-equipment and rebuilding and loans

[52] Sch.4, Pt.I, s.2(a).
[53] H.C. 617-I (1974-5), Q.101.
[54] Cmnd. 6151, para.22.
[55] H.C. 617 (1974-5), para.150.
[56] H.C. 617-I (1974-5), Q.112.
[57] *Ibid.*, Q.57.
[58] H.C. 303 (1974), App.I, para.20 *et seq.*
[59] 860 H.C. Deb., col. 715 *et seq.* (July 19, 1973) as amended by 887 H.C. Deb., col. 212 *et seq.*, Written Answers (February 25, 1975), 904 H.C. Deb., col. 194, Written Answers (January 27, 1976), and *Trade & Industry* December 3, 1976, p.634.

and interest relief grants for more comprehensive restructuring projects as well as grants for the elimination of uneconomic capacity. Similar schemes for the machine tool and ferrous foundry industries provide for concessionary loans towards the development of new machine tools and grants towards approved expenditure on new plant and equipment and new buildings and extensions.[60] The Department is putting great stress on the commercial viability of the projects proposed. Outside advisers have been appointed for these schemes. A scheme for the clothing industry provides for grants for investment in new equipment and other assistance for restructuring and reorganisation both within firms and between firms to improve the productivity and efficiency of the industry. Again emphasis is put on the viability of projects.[61] Another scheme provides assistance mostly in the form of interest relief grants for new capital investment projects which would have been shelved or postponed but for Government help. Emphasis is again placed on the projects being commercially sound and of substantial benefit to the U.K. balance of payments. The aim is to accelerate projects in advance of the expected upturn in world demand.[62]

Secondly, there is an Offshore Supplies Interest Relief Grant scheme for credit obtained to finance contracts for providing British goods and services in the construction of oil platforms.[63] Assistance in the form of interest relief grants has also been provided under s.8 to two offshore projects for the conversion of ships for use in connection with drilling for oil.[64]

RESCUE CASES

All other cases of assistance under s.8 can be classified as rescue operations. In some instances this has taken the form of assistance to facilitate mergers with another company. This happened in the case of the machine tool firm Kearney and Trecker Marwin Ltd.,[65] Scientific and Medical Instruments Ltd.[66] and Norton Villiers Triumph Ltd.,

---

[60] 897 H.C. Deb., col.121, Written Answers (August 5, 1975).
[61] See *Trade and Industry*, October 24, 1975 p.206 and December 10, 1976, p.706. A scheme for the paper and board industries has been announced: *Trade & Industry*, June 18, 1976, p.686, and one for textile and printing machinery makers, *Trade & Industry* August 20, 1976.
[62] *Ibid.*, October 3, 1975, p.2, and November 7, 1975, p.327, and 904 H.C. Deb., col 698 (January 29, 1976). Further schemes have been announced.
[63] 863 H.C. Deb., col.119, Written Answers (November 6, 1973). This scheme is administered by the Offshore Supplies Office, which is part of the Department of Energy.
[64] Annual Report 1974-5, Industry Act 1972, H.C. 620 (1974-5) para.48 and see further H.C. 619 (1975-6), para.54 *et seq.*
[65] For this and later cases see, H.C. 620 (1974-5), para.42, and H.C.619 (1975-6), para.57.
[66] *Trade & Industry*, October 10, 1975, p.69.

the motor cycle firm. As we saw above, in the last case export guarantees were later provided under the same section. Most controversial have been the straightforward rescue operations of British Leyland, where s.8 was used to provide interim assistance, the Meriden co-operative, Alfred Herbert Ltd.,[67] the machine tool firm, and Chrysler. Assistance was also offered under the section to Aston Martin Ltd. but the firm was unable to meet one of the conditions of the offer. These cases raise the same problems of viability as the rescue cases under s.7, such as Govan Shipbuilders Ltd., Cammell Laird Shipbuilders Ltd.,[68] the shipbuilding interests of Court Line Ltd., Bear Brand, the two co-operatives Kirkby Manufacturing Ltd. and Scottish Daily News,[69] Fodens Ltd.,[70] Ferranti Ltd.[71] and Triang Pedigree Ltd.[72] In all these cases considerations other than viability played an important part. Employment considerations, especially in areas of high unemployment were of particular importance. The co-operatives raised other employment considerations being regarded as experiments in industrial organisation. Export considerations were regarded as important in the cases of British Leyland, Chrysler and the Meriden co-operative. Ferranti is not only important for exports but also supplies defence equipment and has high technological capability. Alfred Herbert is Britain's biggest machine tool manufacturer. On the other hand Aston Martin employs a few hundred craftsmen in a non-assisted area making high performance, high fuel consumption, specialty motorcars whose export markets were not assured in the eyes of the Department.[73] As was constantly pointed out in evidence to the Expenditure Committee by the Department, the evaluation of these factors against each other is a matter of judgment for which no precise rules can be formulated.[74] As Mr. Benn pointed out to the same Committee, questions of viability are themselves matters of judgment which one cannot measure with a slide-rule or predict with certainty.[75] Since these decisions are so much matters of judgment the vital issue is whose judgment is decisive and how it is formed.

Even after the reorganisation of the Department of Industry the

[67] 901 H.C. Deb., col. 122, Written Answers (November 25, 1975).
[68] Annual Report 1972-3, Industry Act 1972, H.C. 429 (1972-3), para.15.
[69] *Ibid.,* 1974-5, H.C. 620 (1974-5), para.19 *et seq.*
[70] Fodens were given an interim guarantee but were later rescued by the City.
[71] 892 H.C. Deb., col.457 (May 14, 1975).
[72] *Trade & Industry,* May 23, 1975, p.443.
[73] H.C. 617-I (1974-5), Q.96.
[74] *Ibid.,* Q.112, H.C. 104-ii (1975-6), p.116, paras.18-21, and H.C. 104-ix (1975-6), Q. 2139-41.
[75] H.C. 617-I (1974-5), Q.607. See also H.C. 104-ii (1975-6), paras.17 and 21 — viability should normally be achieved within three years but where the social cost of withholding assistance is particularly high proposals will be given the benefit of the doubt as to prospects of viability.

Government went outside the Department for expert advice in a number of the controversial rescue cases. Most notably in the case of British Leyland, a report was commissioned from Lord Ryder, the Government's industrial adviser, and a team which included members of the Industrial Development Advisory Board.[76] Again, consultants were asked to report on the motor-cycle industry[77] and the Government's decision not to continue support for Norton Villiers Triumph Ltd. was based on this report.[78] In both cases the report was published except for the parts which contained confidential commercial information. Consultants were also appointed in the case of Alfred Herbert Ltd. but their report was not published[79] nor was that relating to the Kirkby co-operative.[80] Another novel feature of these recent cases is the tripartite discussions which took place between the Government, the workforce and the management. Members of Parliament have also been involved in some of the negotiations.

In addition to advice from inside and outside the Department the Industrial Development Advisory Board is normally consulted in these cases though there is no statutory obligation to do so. They were not consulted in the case of Court Line Ltd. because of the time-factor.[81] Where the recommendation of the Board is not accepted by the Secretary of State they can ask him to lay a statement about the matter before Parliament.[82] The advice of the Board was not accepted in the case of the three co-operatives, Bear Brand Ltd.,[83] Chrysler and Alfred Herbert Ltd. They had also advised against assistance to Aston Martin Ltd.[84] In only one case, that is the Kirkby co-operative, did they request the Secretary of State to lay a statement before the House.[85] This was done in the form of a written statement for which the Minister was taken to task.[86] These disagreements gave rise to vigorous criticisms both in the House and before Select Committees. Ministers defended strongly their right to differ from the Board and the civil servants supported them on this point. Mr. Benn put the issue most succinctly when he told the Expenditure Committee: 'It would be quite

---

[76] H.C. 324 (1974-5).

[77] H.C. 532 (1974-5).

[78] 896 H.C. Deb., col. 2059 (July 31, 1975).

[79] 895 H.C. Deb., col. 702 (July 9, 1975). This failure to publish the report was very much criticised by the Opposition.

[80] 885 H.C. Deb., col. 30, Written Answers (January 27, 1975). Coopers & Lybrand advised the Department during the negotiations with Chrysler — H.C. 104-ii (1975-6), Q.203.

[81] 876 H.C. Deb. col. 7-8, Written Answers, (July 1, 1974).

[82] Section 9(4), Industry Act 1972.

[83] *Trade & Industry,* March 28, 1975, p.811.

[84] 884 H.C. Deb., col. 2061 (January 23, 1975).

[85] 883 H.C. Deb., col. 580, Written Answers (December 19, 1974).

[86] 884 H.C. Deb., col. 2052 (January 23, 1975).

wrong to sub-contract decisions to the Advisory Board.'[87] Later he added: 'I think that Ministers must retain the power to take a broader view, a longer-term view, to take account of factors which it would not be right to ask an Industrial Development Advisory Board to deal with.'[88] In a nutshell Mr. Benn is saying that these are political decisions which must be taken by Ministers and cannot be entrusted to any other body. It is precisely for this reason that the Board was made advisory only in contrast to the Board of Trade Advisory Committee which had a veto power over loans and grants under s.4 of the Local Employment Act 1972. The ambit of this committee was progressively whittled down by subsequent legislation[89] until it was finally dissolved under the Industry Act 1972.[90] Later Acts setting up such bodies were careful to give them only advisory functions.[91] In the debates on one of these Bills, the Industrial Expansion Bill, Mr. Benn rejected an amendment which would have given the Committee a power of veto with the same words about 'sub-contracting political decisions' that he later used in evidence to the Expenditure Committee.[92]

Though the Industrial Development Advisory Board have only advisory powers, these are not without effect. As we have seen, the failure to accept their advice in five of the rescue cases led to a political storm in the Commons and much questioning before Select Committees. Though Mr. Benn and the Department staunchly defended these decisions, it is significant that the composition of the Board was enlarged and changed and two industrialists were replaced by two trade unionists.[93] Even more revealing were the remarks of the new Secretary of State, Mr. Varley, when defending his decision not to continue assistance for Norton Villiers Triumph Ltd. by calling in aid the advice of the new Board: 'In the past there have been criticisms that the Board was set up by the previous Conservative administrations and perhaps that was the reason its advice was not followed in all previous cases. Now, however, the Board has been enlarged — some people might say reconstituted — and it has serious trade union leaders as members. No-one would describe them as Right-wing lackeys of British capitalism.'[94] In the debate on the Industrial Expansion Bill just

---

[87] H.C. 617-I (1974-5), Q.587.
[88] *Ibid.,* Q.607.
[89] E.g., Local Employment Act 1963, s.1; Public Expenditure and Receipts Act 1968, s.6.
[90] Sch.2, para. 3(2). It was dissolved on September 30, 1973
[91] Industrial Development Act 1966, s.11; Industrial Expansion Act 1968, s.5.
[92] Standing Committee E, February 20, 1968, col. 109.
[93] *Trade & Industry,* March 14, 1975.
[94] 897 H.C. Deb., col. 775 (August 7, 1975). In the case of Chrysler a clear majority of the Board was prepared to dispense with viability but wanted more stringent conditions — H.C. 104-i (1975-6), p.3, para. 10.

mentioned, Mr. Benn warned that he would be tempted to make political appointments if the Advisory Committee under that Act were given mandatory powers because they would be making political decisions.[95] He succumbed to this temptation in the case of the Industrial Development Advisory Board, even though their powers are far more limited.

The political nature of these decisions is also underlined by the alleged note of reservation filed with regard to the aid for the Kirkby co-operative by the Secretary (Industry), Mr. Carey, the Accounting Officer responsible for this expenditure.[96] The procedure in cases of disagreement between a Minister and the Accounting Officer is laid down in an official publication called 'Government Accounting.'[97] It provides, in Section C paragraph 8:

> '. . . the Accounting Officer is expected to place on record his disagreement with any decision which he considers he would have difficulty in defending before the Public Accounts Committee as a matter of prudent administration. Having done so, he must, if the Minister adheres to the decision, accept it and, if necessary, support his defence of the action taken by reference to the policy ruling of the Minister.
>
> 9. Alternatively the matter of the Accounting Officer's disagreement and his protest may be one which involves his personal accountability on a question of the safeguarding of public funds or the formal regularity or propriety of expenditure. In that case he should state in writing his objection and the reason for it and carry out the Minister's decision only on a written instruction from the Minister overruling his objection. He should then inform the Treasury of the circumstances and communicate the papers to the Comptroller and Auditor General.'

Mr. Carey, in evidence to the Expenditure Committee, categorically denied that he had ever used the procedure under paragraph 9,[98] but when asked whether he regarded the expenditure in relation to the Kirkby co-operative as a proper use of public funds, he refused to be drawn and referred to the confidentiality of the advice given by Civil Servants to Ministers.[99] He then added, 'The answer to your question, Sir John, is that there was a Ministerial decision to give support; and I

---

[95] Standing Committee E, February 20, 1968, col. 108.
[96] See 884 H.C. Deb., col. 79 (January 13, 1975).
[97] See H.C. 393 (1971-2), Q.133.
[98] H.C. 617-I (1974-5), Q.64 *et seq.*
[99] The Minister also refused to be drawn in one of the debates where the allegation was made: 884 H.C. Deb., col. 2058 (January 23, 1975).

accept that decision.'[100] This reply does not rule out the filing of a note of reservation under paragraph 8, as alleged, but it underlines the political nature of the decision.

The political importance of these decisions is also highlighted by the level at which they are made within the Government. As we have seen, important cases, especially those where the Advisory Board's recommendation has not been accepted, usually go to a Cabinet Committee. It is no secret that this committee was later chaired by the Prime Minister.[101] In the case of the rescue of British Leyland the statement was made to the House of Commons by the Prime Minister[102] and Mr. Wilson has been personally involved with Chrysler's application for assistance.[103]

Decisions to refuse assistance or to cut off further assistance, as in the case of Norton Villiers Triumph, are as important as decisions to provide aid. They do not, of course, involve the expenditure of public money and the Treasury would not expect to be consulted in cases the Department wants to turn down.[104] But for the applicants and their employees as well as their suppliers and competitors, the decision is of crucial importance. It is competitors who suffer from decisions to grant aid. It has been said that as a direct consequence of the loan to Bear Brand Ltd. another firm in the hosiery industry collapsed with the loss of 300 jobs.[105] A similar example has been given from the Isle of Mull where an established firm will be forced out of business because of assistance to an incoming firm by the Highlands and Islands Development Board.[106] There is no appeal machinery which can be invoked in such cases at the moment. Both these examples were given to support amendments to the Industry Bill 1975 and the Scottish Development Agency Bill 1975 respectively, designed to prevent unfair competition between the public and the private sector, by setting up an appeal mechanism. The Minister rejected the courts as such an appeal body on the ground that social as well as economic criteria had to be taken into account in deciding unfairness and the courts could not sit in judgment over the exercise of political discretion.[107]

---

[100] H.C. 617-I (1974-5), Q.66.
[101] H.C. 617-I (1974-5), Q.606.
[102] 890 H.C. Deb., col. 1742 (April 24, 1975).
[103] H.C. 596-I (1975-6), Chap V, contains a day-by-day account of the negotiations.
[104] H.C. 617-II (1974-5), Q.2998.
[105] Industry Bill, Standing Committee E, April 15, 1975, col. 756.
[106] 898 H.C. Deb., col. 311 (October 21, 1975). The same point is made in more general terms by the Industrial Development Advisory Board in the Annual Report 1974-5, Industry Act 1972, H.C. 620 (1974-5), p.17.
[107] Industry Bill, Standing Committee E, April 15, 1975, col. 761.

More fundamentally, it was freely conceded by the Government spokesmen in both debates that selective assistance is by nature discriminatory. In particular the preferential purchasing policy towards International Computers Ltd. designed to establish a British computer capability was mentioned.[108] The problem of the preferential treatment of firms which are wholly or partly owned by the Government was anxiously considered by the Expenditure Committee in relation to British Leyland.[109] This raises the whole question of the relationship between such firms and the Government which will be further discussed below. Both selective assistance and preferential treatment of firms in which the Government has a stake involve the weighing of social against economic considerations which has implications not merely for public expenditure but also for private firms who are discriminated against. Whether such discrimination is regarded as unfair or justified by social considerations is a matter of political judgment and underlines the enormous width of discretionary power which the Government wields in this field. In the debate on the Industry Bill 1975 the alleged closure of Volkswagen factories according to the political allegiance of the area in which they were situated was quoted as a warning example.[110] The Minister brushed aside the warning by the assurance that it could not happen here. He put his faith in openness and accountability.[111] When the Industry Bill 1972 was passing through Parliament Mr. Dell was moved to remark how much we depend on the integrity of the Civil Service.[112] We depend perhaps even more heavily on the integrity of our politicians.

CONCLUSION

Government Departments are entrusted with very wide discretionary powers when providing assistance to private industry. Where Parliamentary approval is necessary, the Governmental decision has no legal force but in the vast majority of cases the Government's decision is binding. The procedures for reaching these decisions which have been examined in this chapter do provide some important checks over the exercise of this discretion.

So far as the individual applicant under the Industry Act 1972 is concerned, he is given every assistance with his application so that it

---

[108]   *Ibid.,* col. 759.
[109]   H.C. 617 (1974-5), paras. 292 and 293.
[110]   Standing Committee E, April 15, 1975, col. 764.
[111]   *Ibid.,* col. 768.
[112]   837 H.C. Deb., col. 1096 (May 22, 1972).

stands the best chance of success. The firm negotiates with the Department and will often amend its application to make it acceptable. These procedures are completely informal and contain no legal safeguards but they have received little criticism. An attempt was made during the passage of the Industry Act 1972 through Parliament to give a right of appeal against refusal to a Tribunal and to ensure the giving of reasons.[113] The Minister stated that reasons for refusal were obtainable and rejected an appeal because it would be substituting the Tribunal's decision for that of the Minister. The applicant must, therefore, resort to the political remedy of getting his M.P. to ask a Parliamentary Question or asking him to refer the matter to the Parliamentary Commissioner. Though, as we shall see, there have been a number of such cases concerning investment grants, there has been no such case relating to the selective assistance dealt with in this chapter with the exception of Court Line. But here the complaint was not against the decision to give assistance but the statements made by the Minister in the House of Commons.[114]

The applicant knows the criteria applicable to his case under s.7 where guidelines have been published though the cost per job figure has been kept confidential. These guidelines are not binding on the Minister and he has given aid to firms which do not qualify under them. The Department has not discriminated against firms falling within them but on the contrary has been criticised for not being more flexible and taking into account the applicant's real need for assistance.[115]

The granting of assistance rather than its refusal may lead to discrimination. A firm may, as we have seen, be driven out of business by assistance granted to a competitor. Such a firm has no forum in which to plead its case[116] nor is there any appeal tribunal to which it can complain. Other third parties who may be concerned in an application are the employees of the firm in question. Increasingly they are now brought into the negotiations for discretionary assistance as are M.Ps on behalf of their constituents. Members of the public may also be concerned in a different capacity from that of taxpayer. There is no mechanism for public participation in these decisions though the canvassing of public opinion in the case of major projects has been suggested.

The most important safeguards exist for the protection of public

113 841 H.C. Deb., col. 2443 (July 28, 1972), Report Stage.
114 H.C. 498 (1974-5).
115 H.C. 374 (1974-5), para. 59.
116 It has been suggested by Unilever Ltd. that there should be an opportunity for objections from those likely to be adversely affected: see Memorandum to Expenditure Committee, H.C. 327 (1972-3), p.230, para.3(3).

expenditure. The Treasury has to approve large projects under s.7 and all projects under s.8. The lack of Treasury control in the early stages of Concorde was severely criticised by the Estimates Committee. The Accounting Officer also has the power to object to safeguard public funds or the formal regularity or propriety of expenditure and he can register his disagreement with a decision on the ground of imprudence, but must in such cases accept the policy ruling of the Minister. The expert advice available both within and outside Government Departments is again particularly concerned with prudent expenditure and it was over this issue that the Industrial Development Advisory Board disagreed with the decisions in five of the rescue cases.

The disagreement highlighted the political nature of these decisions. The guidelines for assistance under s.7 can be said to mark the boundary between political and non-political decisions. Cases falling within them are decided by civil servants at regional level though the large cases go to Headquarters and may be decided by a Minister. Cases falling outside them and all cases under s.8, where there are no criteria other than the national interest, involve the balancing of social against economic considerations which is a matter of political judgment that the Government will not entrust to outside bodies or delegate to civil servants in the Department. The decision will, therefore, be made by a Minister or, in important and highly controversial cases, a Cabinet committee or the Cabinet itself. Such a decision will reflect the values of the Minister or Government in power for which they can only be held to account in Parliament as will be discussed below. But such accountability will depend on openness, i.e. publicity of the decision and the evidence on which it is based. As we saw in the last chapter, more decisions are now made public than ever before but the material such as consultants' reports on which they are based are still often confidential.

Though there are virtually no legal safeguards and even the Parliamentary Commissioner has hardly been utilised in this area of wide discretionary power, there are internal and external procedures to ensure that the interests of the applicant and to a much lesser extent those of third parties but in particular the economy of public expenditure are taken into account. But the decision itself will depend on the integrity and values of those who make it.

CHAPTER THREE

NON-SELECTIVE ASSISTANCE UNDER THE INDUSTRY ACT 1972

THE discretion to provide regional development grants under Part I of the Industry Act 1972 is exercised in a totally different way from giving selective assistance under ss. 7 and 8. Not only are the criteria in the Act much more precise but the discretion not to give grants which fall within the criteria is exercised in a very limited way. This is in marked contrast to selective assistance where the criteria in the Act are very wide and the guidelines under s. 7 have no statutory force and therefore do not limit the Secretary of State from going outside them. The guidelines themselves are far less specific than Part I of the Act so that even for cases falling within them there is much more scope for discretion than for regional development grants. Nevertheless the criteria laid down in Part I leave room for the exercise of discretion and the Act gives the Secretary of State complete discretion whether to give grants which fall within its provisions. It was this discretionary nature of the grants which gave rise to considerable controversy when investment grants on which regional development grants were modelled were first introduced in 1966. It is, therefore, necessary to examine first the problems to which these gave rise to see how far they have been solved by the provisions for regional development grants.

INVESTMENT GRANTS

Investment grants were first introduced by the Industrial Development Act 1966. It substituted grants for capital investment in plant and machinery for tax allowances. These grants were made discretionary rather than mandatory and it was round this point that controversy centred in the debates on the Bill. The Opposition wanted the grants made mandatory so that entitlement would be decided by the courts rather than the Minister.[1] They were afraid of the way in which Ministers might exercise their discretion and the enormous power the

---

[1] Standing Committee D, May 24, 1966, col. 35, and 276 H.L. Deb., col. 1214 (August 2, 1966).

Act conferred on them. They were also concerned about the uncertainty for industry which a discretionary power would bring. The Government rejected these amendments on the ground that the courts could not be entrusted with these decisions as they had in *Hinton* v. *Maden*[2] interpreted investment allowances for capital expenditure so widely as to completely destroy the intention of the Act. The courts could only be allowed to make these decisions if the conditions for a grant were very rigidly defined and this would rob the scheme of all flexibility. For similar reasons the Government rejected amendments which would have given a right of appeal against the Minister's decision to a tribunal.[3]

The Minister also argued that instead of an informal helpful attitude towards applicants a mandatory scheme would make everyone look over his shoulder to see if the claim fell within the letter of the law and that an appeal procedure would lead to delay.[4] The internal administrative appeal machinery to the Minister and the mobilisation of M.Ps to bring pressure on the Department can, however, be equally time-wasting.[5]

The Government tried to calm the Opposition's fears about the Act conferring arbitrary discretion on them by saying that 'The Board of Trade has no intention to discriminate between firms because it likes this firm and not that firm, or to make moral judgments, or any judgments of that kind. It can discriminate only according to the type of process carried out or item of equipment or plant which it is considering.'[6] In other words the Department were to be limited to interpreting the Act but this still gave them plenty of scope.

The Act was drawn very widely and contained many terms which needed definition. Although the majority of cases gave rise to no problems there were some difficult border-lines. One of them was the distinction between plant and a building on which investment grants were not payable.[7] This could lead to very fine distinctions in connection with insulation work for cold stores and the Department refined its definitions as the scheme progressed.[8] Similarly, problems arose over the definition of manufacturing which was defined in the Act as the making of an article.[9] Could preparing of animal feed stuffs, grinding[10] or baking be regarded as manufacturing? There were difficulties

[2] [1959] 1 W.L.R. 875.
[3] 732 H.C. Deb., col. 402 (July 19, 1966), and 276 H.L. Deb., col. 1517, (August 4, 1966).
[4] 732 H.C. Deb., col. 410 (July 19, 1966).
[5] 276 H.L. Deb., col. 1222 (August 2, 1966).
[6] Standing Committee D, May 24, 1966, col. 48.
[7] *cf.* Regional Development Grants.
[8] H.C. 290 (1972-3), p. 165, Case No. C.20/G — Fourth Report of P.C.A.
[9] Section 1(2a)
[10] See H.C. 406 (1972-3), p. 196, Case No. C.460/G — Fifth Report of P.C.A.

where machinery was used partly for a qualifying process and partly not.[11] The equipment also had to be used for the manufacturing process or incidental to it. Thus, the directors' cocktail cabinet and office and canteen equipment which had made the investment allowance scheme so non-discriminatory were excluded. In addition, it was the Department rather than the Inland Revenue Tribunals and the courts who drew the distinction between capital and revenue expenditure. This gave rise to problems in connection with reconditioning machines by replacement of parts.[12] The Department adopted a more restrictive policy after some months.

This tremendous flexibility would have been impossible if these grants had been made mandatory instead of discretionary or if there had been an appeal to a tribunal. It would have been impossible for the Department to change its mind as easily as the scheme progressed and thus to keep it in line with policy objectives. The way in which the Act was administered clearly showed the advantages from the Government's point of view of leaving discretion to interpret the Act in the Department. However, these administrative advantages did create problems for the individual. Applicants were given guidance in a booklet 'Guide for Industry' which was revised after one year but this could not cover every case and its wording was sometimes ambiguous.[13] Also, in the early cases, expenditure was incurred before guidance was issued.[14] But the biggest problem was created by changes in policy which could mislead those who had relied on a less restrictive policy into incurring expenditure which was later disallowed. It was in these cases that the Parliamentary Commissioner for Administration could sometimes provide a remedy.

The P.C.A. very firmly refused to act as a court of appeal from the Department on questions of eligibility.[15] He regarded such issues as matters of policy of which he could not question the merits.[16] But, under his extended jurisdiction to question 'bad rules,' he could and did ask the Department to reconsider a rule which caused hardship but once this had been done he could not query their decision to adhere to their rule. This is what happened in the case of the revised policy about reconditioned machines.[17] In this case the Department

---

[11] *Ibid.* — 50 per cent or more was used as the yardstick.
[12] H.C. 138 (1969-70), p. 127, Case No. C.379/68 — Second Report of P.C.A.
[13] H.C. 290 (1972-3), p. 165, Case No. C.20/G.
[14] H.C. 138 (1969-70), p. 127, Case No. C.379/68.
[15] H.C. 290 (1972-73), p. 165, Case No.C.20/G.
[16] H.C. 334 (1971-2), Q.293 — Second Report from Select Committee on P.C.A.
[17] H.C. 138 (1969-70), p. 127, Case No. C.379/68.

also devised a transitional policy for those whose claims were outstanding when the policy was changed which caused hardship to some applicants who had incurred expenditure in reliance on the old policy. The Department, after reviewing this transitional policy, decided to suspend it but refused to do so retrospectively. This again precluded the P.C.A. from questioning their decision further but the Select Committee probed the matter in depth though they made no recommendation in their report.[18]

In this case there was no remedy for the hardship caused by a change of policy to the complainant but in other cases the P.C.A. was able to obtain redress. If the applicant had been misled by statements of the Department and had incurred expenditure as a result he obtained compensation.[19] But the mere fact that grants had previously been paid in error[20] or because the policy had not yet been clarified[21] would not entitle the applicant to further grants though in these cases no attempt was made to recover the grants already paid. It was the normal practice of the Department not to recover grants paid under the policy as previously interpreted but to recover grants paid in error unless the error was contributed to by ambiguity on the part of the Department.[22]

It is clear, therefore, that the tremendous flexibility with which investment grants were administered did give rise to problems for applicants who were not always clear what criteria would be applied and were confronted by changes of policy and interpretation. Though there were cases of hardship for which there was no remedy, the P.C.A. obtained redress in a number of cases and also ensured that changes of policy in the future would not be detrimental to those who had incurred expenditure under the old policy.[23] The P.C.A., therefore, played an important part in ensuring that administrative convenience was not pursued at the expense of the individual.

The discretion of the Department was not limited to interpretation of the terms of the Act. It was also possible for the Department in the exercise of their discretion to lay down a minimum limit below which an item would not be eligible for grant. The Opposition tried unsuccessfully in the House of Lords to have this limit fixed by an order rather than pure administrative discretion,[24] but the Government wished to preserve the maximum flexibility. The limit was fixed at £25

[18] H.C. 240 (1970-1), p.40 *et seq.* — First Report from Select Committee on P.C.A.
[19] H.C. 138 (1969-70), p.137, Case No. C.640/68.
[20] H.C. 290 (1972-3), p.165, Case No. C.20/G.
[21] H.C. 406 (1972-3), p.196, Case No. C.460/G.
[22] H.C. 116 (1971-2), p.320, Case No. C.203/B, and H.C. 42 (1973-4), p.170, Case No. C.98/T.
[23] H.C. 138 (1969-70), p.127, Case No. C.379/68.
[24] 276 H.L. Deb., col. 1253 (August 2, 1966).

and it was this exercise of discretion which was challenged in the courts.

In *British Oxygen Co. Ltd.* v. *Minister of Technology*[25] the plaintiff asked *inter alia* for a declaration that the Board of Trade was not entitled to decline to make a grant towards bulk expenditure on gas cylinders each of which cost £20. Buckley J.[26] granted the declaration. He regarded refusal to consider grants below £25 as an abrogation rather than an exercise of discretion and thought that low individual cost could not 'be so weighty and conclusive a consideration . . . as to make all other considerations irrelevant.'[27] The Court of Appeal reversed his decision on this point[28] and their decision was upheld by the House of Lords. Lord Reid, like the Court of Appeal, drew the distinction between adopting a policy and refusing to hear a case: 'What the authority must not do is to refuse to listen at all. But a Ministry or large authority may have had to deal already with a multitude of similar applications and then they will almost certainly have evolved a policy so precise that it could well be called a rule. There can be no objection to that, provided the authority is always willing to listen to anyone with something new to say . . .'[29] Lord Dilhorne went further when he said: 'It seems pointless and a waste of time that the Board should have to consider applications which are bound as a result of its policy decision to fail. Representations could of course be made that the policy be changed.'[30] This approach seems to be more in line with administrative reality. The House of Lords categorically affirmed the intention of the Legislature that grants were discretionary and that the Board of Trade was under no duty to make a grant to anyone who was eligible under the Act.[31] Lord Reid left open two general grounds on which the discretion could be attacked, namely bad faith and unreasonableness, which showed there had been no genuine exercise of discretion.[32] The House of Lords' decision, therefore, virtually made the Minister's discretion judgeproof.

[25] [1970] 3 W.L.R. 488, H.L.
[26] [1968] 3 W.L.R. 1.
[27] At p.15B
[28] [1969] 2 W.L.R. 877, 887D and 889H. The declaration granted referred to declining a grant not refusal to consider an application.
[29] [1970] 3 W.L.R. 488, 495B.
[30] At p.500E.
[31] At p.493H and 499D.
[32] At p.494D.

REGIONAL DEVELOPMENT GRANTS

Though investment grants were abolished by the Investment and Building Grants Act 1971, they were resuscitated in an amended form as regional development grants by Part I of the Industry Act 1972. These are payable only in assisted areas but are available for buildings as well as new machinery or plant. The criterion for eligibility is if the grant is for 'qualifying premises' which are defined as premises wholly or mainly used for 'qualifying activities,' such as manufacturing, mining and construction.[33] This change was intended to make payment of the grants more certain and predictable.[34] Whether it has achieved this purpose will now be examined.

The C.B.I., giving evidence to the Expenditure Committee soon after the introduction of regional development grants, claimed that they were less predictable than investment grants and that most cases were now marginal.[35] They again called for mandatory grants and an appeal procedure[36] and this was echoed by firms such as Ford,[37] Vauxhall[38] and I.C.I.[39] This plea was again rejected by the Department on the ground that this would lead to inflexibility and delay.[40] The Department thought that the C.B.I's view was due to lack of familiarity with the new system and would change when the period of transition was complete.[41]

Applications for Regional Development Grant are dealt with by four Regional Development Grant offices headed by an Assistant Secretary. They are issued with detailed instructions by Headquarters and will refer there any cases which do not fall within those guidelines.[42] The C.B.I. criticised the delay, pettiness and lack of co-ordination of the departmental machinery but they acknowledged that these might be teething troubles[43] and the Department confidently expected the time for processing a claim to be reduced below six weeks as the scheme became established.[44] Similarly, they expected the number of civil servants required to administer the scheme to be one-half of those

---

[33] Industry Act 1972, ss. 1 and 2. Mining and Construction are no longer 'qualifying activities' — S.I. 1976 No. 1573.
[34] 837 H.C. Deb., col. 1016 (May22, 1972).
[35] H.C. 327 (1972-3), Q.1946.
[36] *Ibid.*, p.376, para. 20.
[37] *Ibid.*, p.84.
[38] *Ibid.*, p.467.
[39] *Ibid.*, p.508.
[40] *Ibid.*, Q.2028.
[41] H.C. 303 (1974), Q.69, p.12 (Evidence to the Public Accounts Committee).
[42] *Ibid.*, Qs. 16 and 17.
[43] H.C. 327 (1972-3), Q.1946.
[44] H.C. 303 (1974), Q.79, p.13.

needed for dealing with investment grants.[45]

The Department has issued notes for guidance which have been revised in the light of experience.[46] The main difficulty lies in defining 'qualifying premises.' The C.B.I. criticised in particular the Department's treatment of separate buildings[47] but the Department regarded their criticism as directed at the Act rather than its interpretation.[48] Whether premises are wholly or mainly used for qualifying activities depends usually[49] on whether the majority of employees are so engaged which was again criticised by the C.B.I.[50] but this once more is inherent in the legislation. In spite of these difficulties of interpretation the new system should be easier to administer because once the premises have been found to qualify within the Act repeat applications for the same premises can be dealt with more quickly. Also, when examining claims it is only necessary to ensure that the asset is used on the premises, whereas previously it had to be used for a qualifying process.[51]

So far, we have been considering the Secretary of State's discretion in interpreting the Act, which was the main reason for not making the grants mandatory, but he has also used his discretion to make general rules about eligibility. Thus, grant is not paid on furniture or assets provided for recreational purposes because it is difficult to control the location of the asset and because it is non-functional and not within the spirit of the Act.[52] Certain bodies such as local authorities, universities, other educational bodies and bodies which are substantially assisted by the Government, have also been excluded from the scheme.[53] Again, this discretion has been used to fix a minimum figure of £100 for plant and machinery and £1,000 for buildings below which no grant will be paid.[54] This rule, which, as we saw, was upheld by the courts in the context of investment grants, was justified on grounds of administrative convenience and ease of enforcing their use on qualifying premises. The motor industry, who were at first highly critical of this limit, later retracted their strictures.[55]

It is very interesting that the Secretary of State has not used his discretion in the reverse way to cut down the grant where the project is

---

[45] *Ibid.,* Q.21, p.5.
[46] *Ibid.,* Q.44, p.9.
[47] H.C. 327 (1972-3), p.375, para. 19.
[48] *Ibid.,* Q.2028.
[49] For alternative criteria, see H.C. 303 (1974), Q.86 *et seq.,* p.14.
[50] H.C. 327 (1972-3), Q.1946.
[51] H.C. 303 (1974), Q.72, p.12.
[52] *Ibid.,* Q.57 *et seq.,* p.11.
[53] *Ibid.,* Q.47, p.10, and App. I, para. 11.
[54] These general rules were announced in the White Paper, Cmnd. 4942, preceding the Bill.
[55] H.C. 303 (1974), Q.84, p.14.

very large. Though the then Secretary of State suggested during the passage of the Bill that his discretion could be so used in very large cases,[56] the Department told the Public Accounts Committee that the discretion would not be used for this purpose.[57] This illustrates very well the limited way in which the Department has so far used its discretion and that the fears about the arbitrary use of discretion voiced by the Opposition when investment grants were introduced have so far proved unjustified. It is also revealing that, so far, the Parliamentary Commissioner has not been asked to deal with complaints against regional development grants which may be an indication that some lessons have been learnt from the investment grant scheme.

CONCLUSION

The administration of investment and regional development grants by the Department of Industry shows the immense flexibility which is feasible when discretionary authority is conferred on a Government Department. Such flexibility would be impossible if authority were vested in the courts or tribunals. Though the discretion has been used almost exclusively to define eligibility for grants, there is a price to pay for this great flexibility and it is paid by the individual. The ability of the Department to change its mind about definitions as the scheme progressed could work hardship to firms who were relying on past practice and who could be asked to repay grants paid in error. The P.C.A., as we have seen, can mitigate hardship in some of these cases but it is not surprising that the administration of the Act has encountered much criticism from firms on the grounds of unpredictability, complexity and delay.[58] This may be a necessary price to pay for making the grants sufficiently discriminatory.

The provision of grants in contradistinction to investment allowances raises even more fundamental questions of decision-making. We are not so much concerned here with the substantive differences over which controversy has raged, such as whether cash grants are more immediately beneficial to firms than taxation of profits.[59] The most important difference is the way in which grants and tax allowances are regarded ideologically. Grants are treated as a discretionary

[56] 841 H.C. Deb., col. 2366-8 (July 28, 1972).
[57] H.C. 303 (1974), Q.55, p.11.
[58] For a good example of such criticism see the case quoted by Dunlop Ltd. in their evidence to the Trade and Industry Sub-committee on Regional Development Incentives: H.C. 327 (1972-3), App. 6, p.492. See also *ibid.*, p.306 (Courtaulds Ltd.), p.467 (Vauxhall Ltd.) and p.485 (Cadbury Schweppes Ltd.).
[59] For a summary of conflicting views, see H.C.85 (1973-4), para.41.

hand-out tinged with charity whereas allowances are regarded as a retention of the firm's own money *vis a vis* the tax-gatherer. Grants can be quantified to show that industry is subsidised at the rate of £2 million per day.[60] This argument can be countered by the tax bill which industry pays back to the State but this does not give information about tax allowances. The lack of information about depreciation allowances was much regretted by the Trade and Industry sub-committee of the Expenditure Committee which elicited from the Department that the reduction of information to Parliament had not been taken into account when the changeover from investment grants to depreciation allowances was made in 1970.[61] The Chairman of the Trade and Industry sub-committee made the point that allowances involve the expenditure of public money as much as grants.[62] This point has been driven home by a later report of the Expenditure Committee which for the first time received evidence about the cost of tax allowances.[63] This led one M.P. on the committee to make the same point about indiscriminate hand-outs to industry which has in the past been made in relation to subsidies. It does seem that there is now more awareness of the relation between tax allowances and subsidies for the purpose of public expenditure and if looked at in this light it is difficult to justify their being treated differently either ideologically or administratively.

In the context of regional development policy, grants and allowances represent the carrot to attract industry — the stick is contained in industrial development certificates which have to be obtained for industrial development above certain limits outside the assisted areas. Again, it is revealing to contrast regional grants with I.D.Cs as they are different mechanisms to achieve the same end. The procedure for granting I.D.Cs is similar to that for grants and the same suggestions have been made to formalise it by setting up an appeal tribunal. The Hunt Committee on the Intermediate Areas reported against establishing such a procedure on the grounds that it could not operate with the flexibility and sensitivity of the present system.[64] They did, however, recognise that the procedure could be burdensome for small firms who were less well-equipped for dealing with officials. Really small firms will, however, not be affected by I.D.C. policy as they will fall within the exemption limits of I.D.Cs.[65]

It is the medium-sized firm which is most affected by I.D.C. policy,

[60] 873 H.C. Deb., col. 539, Written Answers (May 16, 1974).
[61] H.C. 347 (1971-2), para. 279.
[62] *Ibid.*, Minutes of Evidence, Vol. II, Q.146 *et seq.*
[63] H.C. 299 (1975-6), para. 12, and Appendix.
[64] (1969) Cmnd. 3998, paras. 484-5.
[65] See H.C. 327 (1972-3), App. 10, para. 6. But note that the exemption limits have since been increased.

as was graphically illustrated by the evidence given to the Trade and Industry Sub-Committee of the Expenditure Committee by the Reliant Motor Co. whose expansion was halted for several years by refusal of an I.D.C. because it could not afford to expand in a new area.[66] By contrast, large firms can in effect buy I.D.Cs by doing a deal with the Department and offering to expand in a development area in return for an I.D.C. in a non-assisted area.[67]

The most important contrast between I.D.Cs and grants as instruments of regional development is that there is no compensation for refusal of an I.D.C. The extent to which such refusals bring pressure to bear on firms to expand in development areas varies, as we have seen, with the firm.[68] Where it does have this effect regional incentives do offset some of the costs of moving to a development area but the Expenditure Committee received a great deal of evidence that regional aid did not compensate firms in the long term for such a move.[69] This evidence was countered by the Department[70] but precise figures are not available and the Department thought it was not feasible to tailor regional assistance exactly to each project. The evidence does seem to show, however, that large firms were rarely induced to expand by incentives though more frequently it affected the choice of location. Smaller firms, were, however, more influenced by financial inducements.[71]

It would seem, therefore, from the evidence available, that neither the stick nor the carrot technique for regional development affects the small firm in non-development areas.[72] At the other end of the spectrum the large firms with plants all over the country were well-cushioned against the stick and regarded incentives as sugar on the pill or gilt on the gingerbread depending on the circumstances. It is in this context that one must look at proposals for planning agreements.[73] These were modelled on the development agreement or programme contract system used in Italy, France and Belgium. In Italy, leading firms submit their major investment and job programmes over five years on a rolling annual basis to the Ministry of the Budget where they are assessed for regional implications. Location is then negotiated between the firms and the Ministry and the firms then obtain

---

[66] *Ibid.*, Q.263 *et seq.*
[67] H.C. 85 (1973-74), paras. 31(d) and 36, and H.C. 617-I (1974-5), Q.40.
[68] For a summary of the views of the firms who gave evidence to the Trade and Industry Sub-Committee, see H.C.85 (1973-4), para. 30 *et seq.*
[69] *Ibid.*, para. 32 *et seq.*
[70] H.C. 327 (1972-3), p.413 *et seq.*, and see H.C. 104-ii (1975-6), Q.426 *et seq.*
[71] H.C. 85 (1973-4), Chap. 3.
[72] H.C. 327 (1972-3), App. 10, para. 7.
[73] Cmnd. 5710 — White Paper on the Regeneration of British Industry and Consultative Document of the Department of Industry: see *Trade and Industry*, August 8, 1975.

their regional incentives.[74] Planning agreements will be negotiated only with major firms in key sectors of manufacturing industry and in selected industries other than manufacturing of particular importance and including the Nationalised Industries and publicly-owned firms. Consultations will take place annually. The Government will assess with the company its needs for assistance especially for development in the regions. The Government will agree with the company the scale and purpose of selective assistance which will meet the needs of the individual firm. When a planning agreement exists, aid may not fall below the existing rates during the currency of the agreement[75] which will remove the lack of continuity of such assistance which is the main complaint about aid made by industry at the moment.[76] By this means it is hoped to ensure that government financial assistance is deployed where it will be most effectively used. The agreements will not be legally binding contracts and the machinery for consultation will not differ markedly from existing procedures for negotiating I.D.Cs and grants. The difference will be in harmonising the plans of the companies with national objectives and tailoring the assistance to the needs of the firm on a much more coherent, certain and comprehensive basis than hitherto.

[74] H.C. 85-I (1973-4), p.690.
[75] Industry Act 1975, s.21.
[76] H.C. 85 (1973-4), para. 16 *et seq.*

CHAPTER FOUR

INDEPENDENT AGENCIES

IN this chapter we will examine the part played by independent agencies in providing public money for private industry. Some of the bodies discussed are no longer in existence, whilst others have been newly-established. By this means it is hoped to clarify the role which such independent bodies can play in this field.

SHIPBUILDING INDUSTRY BOARD

This Board was set up under the Shipbuilding Industry Act 1967 to implement the recommendations of the Geddes Committee for the reorganisation of the shipbuilding industry by merging existing companies into groups. The Board was intended to be temporary and, after having its life extended for one year, was dissolved on December 31, 1971.[1] It had power to make grants to undertakings which were involved in a reorganisation scheme and to make loans for capital investment.[2] Both grants and loans were subject to the approval of the Minister. In practice this approval was always forthcoming. In fact the Minister most concerned, Mr. Benn, is on record as saying that he never found reason to dissent from the judgment of the S.I.B.[3] This did not, however, mean that they always saw eye to eye and perhaps the relationship was more aptly characterised by the Permanent Secretary who said that it varied from time to time due to the personalities involved but that, 'in general the S.I.B. was regarded very much as the front runner of the operation.'[4]

The initiative undoubtedly lay with the S.I.B. The Board did the negotiating and assessment which would otherwise have been done in the Department and the Department firmly took the view that it was wrong to set up the Board and then do the job itself.[5] It would

---

[1] S.I. 1971 No. 1939.
[2] Shipbuilding Industry Act 1967, s.3 (as amended by Industrial Expansion Act 1968 s.10) and s.4.
[3] H.C. 397 (1968-9), Q.1438 — Report of Select Committee on Scottish Affairs.
[4] H.C. 447 (1971-2), Q.1222 — Third Report of Public Accounts Committee.
[5] H.C. 397 (1968-9), Q.1413.

sometimes cross-check by having another look at a proposal within the Department[6] but in the case of the Upper Clyde Shipbuilders merger the Department made no further investigations even though the S.I.B. had mentioned its misgivings about the merger.[7] When this group was later granted further aid, the Minister had no part in the conditions laid down and never discussed in detail the precise percentage of the Government shareholding. In fact he said that he only learnt of earlier rescue plans from the press.[8] However, when the S.I.B. refused to provide further assistance to U.C.S. out of the funds available to it under the Act, the Government provided a £7 million loan to prevent massive unemployment.[9] As Mr. Benn said, he was bound to take into account the wider social and economic considerations which the Board were not entitled to consider.[10] The Minister was, therefore, mistaken when he said on an earlier occasion that he had no statutory powers to provide assistance to the shipbuilding industry outside the recommendations of the S.I.B.[11] The money was provided by means of a Supplementary Estimate and this was also the way assistance was provided in the case of Cammell Laird Shipbuilders Ltd. where the powers of the S.I.B. under the 1967 Act were not appropriate.[12] In these cases, therefore, the Government had to intervene directly because the powers of the Board were inadequate. One may wonder whether the Chairman of the Board's verdict that the Board was an 'independent means of judging and looking at these situations free from any conflict of interest'[13] is a euphemism for saying that it could not take political decisions.

Once money had been committed by the S.I.B., it had to decide whether to put a nominee on the board of the company and such a nominee would then report back to the Board.[14] The S.I.B. acted as a buffer between the industry and the Department so that the latter had to press its views, for example on the renegotiation of contracts, on the industry through the S.I.B. and was not getting detailed information back from the firm.[15] Conversely, the chairmen of the shipbuilding firms complained of the lack of direct contact with the Government

[6] H.C. 447 (1971-2), Q.1265.
[7] *Ibid.*, Q.1279 *et seq.*
[8] H.C. 397 (1968-9), Q.1447 *et seq.*
[9] 793 H.C. Deb., col. 662 *et seq.* (December 11, 1969).
[10] H.C. 347 (1971-2), vol. II, Q.454-6, and H.C. 447 (1971-2), para. 10.
[11] H.C. 397 (1968-9), Q.1412.
[12] 801 H.C. Deb., col. 590 (May 7, 1970).
[13] H.C. 347 (1971-2), Vol. II, Q.562.
[14] In the case of U.C.S., the S.I.B. director also reported to the Government from the time that Government money was committed, see H.C.347 (1971-2), Vol. III, Q.2113.
[15] H.C. 447 (1971-2), Q.1315.

because of the existence of the Board.[16] The one thing that the former chairmen of U.C.S. and Fairfields seemed to agree on was that the S.I.B. was more of a hindrance than a help.[17] It was, therefore, not, to use the words of its chairman, 'a most effective bridge'[18] between Government and industry but a road-block. It enabled the Government to shuffle off responsibility for effectively monitoring the expenditure of public money[19] without absolving them from the ultimate political responsibility of deciding whether to salve the wreckage of U.C.S. from the crash the S.I.B. had been powerless to prevent.

INDUSTRIAL REORGANISATION CORPORATION

The Industrial Reorganisation Corporation (I.R.C.) was created by statute in 1966 with powers under s.2(1) (*a*) to promote or assist the reorganisation or the development of any industry and (*b*) if requested by the Secretary of State to establish or develop any industrial enterprise. The I.R.C. had £150 million of public money to spend in the form of loans and it had the power to acquire equity but it had no powers of compulsory acquisition. Unlike the S.I.B. there was no requirement for Ministerial approval of individual loans. The Minister had power to give general directions but no such directions were ever given.[20] However, on a number of occasions the I.R.C. were asked to undertake projects for the Government. It was asked to examine the tenders for the aluminium smelters. It was also asked to assess the financial position of Cunards and to study the relationship of the Post Office and the telecommunications industry.[21] Again, it was asked to implement the reorganisation of the nuclear power industry and the consolidation of the trawling fleet industry.[22] These projects, undertaken at the suggestion of the Government, fell within the general powers of the corporation under s.2(1)(*a*).

Assistance to a particular firm as distinct from aiding reorganisation of several firms could only be undertaken at the request of the Secretary of State under s.2(1)(b). Such requests were made in the case of Rolls-Royce and Cammell Laird Ltd. which, in the latter case, was reluctantly accepted by the I.R.C. who did not want to

[16] H.C. 347 (1971-2), Vol. III, Q.2113 (Mr. Hepper), and Q.2276 (Mr. Stewart).
[17] *Ibid.*, Q.2178 and Q.2254.
[18] *Ibid.*, Vol.II, Q.563.
[19] This point is well made by Dell, *op. cit.*, p.166 *et seq.*
[20] S.2(5) This is similar to the position in the Nationalised Industries.
[21] H.C. 252 (1967-8), para. 6.
[22] H.C. 286 (1968-9), p.11.

get involved in shipbuilding.[23] It was also at the request of the Government that the I.R.C. was asked to intervene in the Rootes-Chrysler deal to ensure that the Government obtained a share in the company.[24] The I.R.C. could have refused such requests but in practice the relationship with Government departments was one of close co-operation and it was acting within the framework of Government policy. But it was free to make its own decisions on individual projects without being subject to a Government veto[25] and its operational independence was scrupulously respected by the Government which neither insisted on nor prevented any course of action.[26] The former chairman of the I.R.C. is on record as saying that it was never subject to political pressures.[27]

In fact the boot seems to have been on the other foot. The I.R.C. took the initiative in restructuring industry to the extent of not only acting as catalyst but as accelerator in the case of the G.E.C./A.E.I. merger and as steersman in the G.E.C./E.E. merger. It intervened directly in support of George Kent in another merger and purchased Brown Bayley Ltd. to facilitate restructuring of the ball-bearings industry.[28] It was this active role of direct intervention in the market place that caused the first managing director to resign[29] and occasioned political unease at the Board's power and independence[30] which led to its abolition by the incoming Government in 1971.[31] The exercise of the merger function not only led to the I.R.C's untimely death, it also enabled the Government during the Board's lifetime to shuffle off responsibility for reconciling its policies on monopolies and restrictive practices with that on concentration of industry.[32]

In retrospect, the former managing director of the Corporation regretted that the I.R.C. had not concentrated more on selective investment rather than mergers.[33] This is the function which was given to the Department of Industry by the Industry Act 1972. As we have seen, the recruitment of businessmen to serve in the Department to some extent met the argument that a Board consisting of industrialists is more competent to make commercial judgments. Another argument in favour of an independent agency for this task is that of continuity

[23] H.C. 447 (1971-2), Q.1191.
[24] H.C. 252 (1967-8), para. 5(iii).
[25] *Ibid.*, para. 2.
[26] H.C. 286 (1968-9), p.9.
[27] H.C. 347 (1971-2), vol. III, Q.1821.
[28] H.C. 286 (1968-9), p.8.
[29] H.C. 347 (1971-2), vol. II, Q.1251.
[30] *Ibid.*, vol. III, Q.1807.
[31] Industry Act 1971.
[32] H.C. 347 (1971-2), vol. II, Q.1262.
[33] *Ibid.*, vol. III, Q.1807.

which is the counterpart of political independence. As is graphically illustrated by the life and death of the I.R.C., continuity and independence are only possible in the case of an agency if it is taken out of the political arena and enjoys the support of both political parties.[34] If there develops a consensus about the existence of such a body it can act as a political buffer which may sometimes be a euphemism for shuffling off responsibility. But in the last resort the Government will have to take political decisions such as whether to establish an aluminium smelting industry or to rescue Rolls-Royce.

THE NATIONAL ENTERPRISE BOARD

The Government had learnt lessons from the I.R.C. by the time the N.E.B. was established. It originated as an instrument for extending nationalisation into the profitable sections of private industry to enable the Government to control prices, stimulate investment, encourage exports, create employment, protect the public from multinational companies and plan the economy.[35] By the time the White Paper on 'The Regeneration of British Industry'[36] was published there were no provisions for compulsory acquisition except with specific Parliamentary approval in the case of loss to unacceptable foreign control of an important manufacturing undertaking. These provisions were embodied in the Industry Act 1975.[37]

There was a great deal of controversy over what was meant by acquisition of shares 'by agreement' which was the phrase used in the White Paper.[38] The Opposition were very concerned that this should include the agreement of the directors as well as the shareholders and unsuccessfully moved an amendment to this effect.[39] By the time of the third reading the Government made a concession that the guidelines for the Board, which are given effect by a direction under s.7 of the Industry Act 1975, would require the N.E.B. to inform the Secretary of State before acquiring more than 10 per cent of the shares of a company without the consent of the directors and he could ask them not to proceed. The guidelines implemented this pledge.[40] There was no such restriction on the I.R.C.

The N.E.B. was also made subject to closer ministerial control in other respects. Section 10 of the Industry Act 1975 provides that the

[34] This point was well made by Sir Frank Schon, *ibid.*, Q.1860 and Q.1871.
[35] Labour Party Manifesto, 1974 (February).
[36] Cmnd. 5710.
[37] Sections 11-20.
[38] Para. 31.
[39] Standing Committee E, col. 418 (March 25, 1975).
[40] *Trade and Industry*, December 24, 1976.

consent of the Secretary of State will be necessary before the N.E.B. or any of its subsidiaries can acquire share capital entitling it to exercise 30 per cent or more of the votes or if the cost of the acquisition exceeds £10 million. The guidelines provide that the Secretary of State has given a general authority to subsidiaries to acquire more than 30 per cent of the share capital if this is not opposed by the company and the cost does not exceed £½ million. In the case of disposal of shares where there are no statutory provisions for the Secretary of State's consent, the guidelines make his approval necessary except in the case of shares not exceeding £½ million by subsidiaries.

Again, as in the case of the I.R.C., there are no statutory provisions for the N.E.B. to obtain approval for giving assistance to firms but the guidelines make the Secretary of State's consent obligatory for projects over £25 million and the N.E.B. must give him advance notice in all cases over £10 million so that he can intervene if he thinks fit. In this context it is important that he can give the Board specific as well as general directions under s.7 of the Industry Act 1975 which again provides for closer ministerial control than in the case of the I.R.C.[41]

The most crucial provision in this context is s.3 of the Industry Act 1975 which enables the Secretary of State with the consent of the Treasury to direct the N.E.B. to exercise as his agent his powers of giving selective assistance under ss.7 and 8 of the Industry Act 1972.[42] The Secretary of State must reimburse the N.E.B. for any assistance granted under such a direction.[43] This section may be regarded as the lame duck provision because it is under this section that rescue cases will be dealt with rather than under the general powers of the Board. This is crucial to the functioning and *raison d'etre* of the Board. By retaining the most controversial political decisions, i.e. the rescue cases within the Government's own control the confusion of responsibility which arose over U.C.S. and Rolls-Royce should be avoided. Political responsibility for rescue cases will remain squarely with the Government and it will not be able to pass the buck or shuffle off responsibility to the N.E.B.

Though responsibility for rescue cases should be clear-cut, it will not always be possible to draw a hard and fast line between social and commercial considerations. The N.E.B. has as its subsidiaries firms which have been rescued and which will require further injections of public money. Some of this will be provided by the Department under

---

[41] Directions must be laid before Parliament or reasons given for failure to do so — Industry Act 1975, s.7(3).

[42] After giving such a direction the Secretary of State has to lay before Parliament a statement giving particulars of the assistance to be provided by the N.E.B.

[43] Sections 3 (10)-(13).

ss.7 and 8 of the Industry Act 1972 but it is also envisaged that the N.E.B. will provide some from its fund of £700 million.[44] The Secretary of State may determine different financial duties for different assets and activities of the N.E.B.[45] and the guidelines envisage that the Government will settle individual objectives for holdings in very large companies such as Rolls-Royce and British Leyland.

Though it is the duty of the Secretary of State to satisfy himself that the financial duties imposed on the Board are likely, taken together, to result in an adequate return on capital,[46] the N.E.B. has wider objectives than a commercial enterprise. One of the statutory functions of the Board is the provision, maintenance or safeguarding of employment.[47] The guidelines provide that the N.E.B. must consider expansion or new development in a development area if possible and it will expect this of its subsidiaries other things being equal. Rolls-Royce is expressly charged with a duty to examine such locations in the concordat between itself and the N.E.B.[48]

This will not be the only way in which the N.E.B. will fulfil its role to create employment. Through regional offices in areas of high unemployment it will be expected to play an active part in seeking out worthwhile proposals for investment by the N.E.B. and put them in hand either in co-operation with private industry or by itself. It is this active, entrepreneurial role which distinguishes the N.E.B. from the Department exercising its powers under s.7 of the Industry Act 1972. Though the Department does have a promotional role,[49] it is in the last resort dependent on firms coming forward with applications[50] and cannot by direct action establish an undertaking or promote a joint enterprise with private industry. By this means the N.E.B. will discharge in the English development areas the same functions as the Scottish, Welsh and Northern Ireland Development Agencies and the Highlands and Islands Development Board perform in their regions.[51]

The most controversial function of the N.E.B. is that of extending

---

[44] Industry Act 1975, s.8(2). This can be raised with the consent of the Treasury to £1,000 million by an order subject to approval by the House of Commons (s.8(3)).
[45] Industry Act 1975, s.6(1).
[46] Industry Act 1975, s.6(3).
[47] Industry Act 1975 s.2(1)(c).
[48] Memorandum of Understanding about the relationship between N.E.B. and RR 71.
[49] H.C. 327 (1972-3), Q.518.
[50] H.C. 617-I (1974-5), Q.18.
[51] The wording of the respective Acts is slightly different, however. Whilst the Industry Act, s.2(2)(a) provides for the establishing of an industrial undertaking by the N.E.B., the Development Agencies are all given express powers to carry on industrial undertakings — see Scottish Development Agency Act 1975, s.2(2)(b), Highlands and Islands Development (Scotland) Act, 1965, s.6, The Industries Development (Northern Ireland) Order 1976, S.I. 1976 No. 580, s.4(2)(a), Welsh Development Agency Act 1975, s.1(3)(c).

public ownership into profitable areas of manufacturing industry,[52] a function which is not given to any of the development agencies. But, as we have seen, the N.E.B. has no powers of compulsory acquisition so that it will have to find willing sellers to exercise these powers. It will be able to go into the market to bid for shares but this is likely to be an expensive business once it becomes known that the N.E.B. is interested and any acquisition over 10 per cent against the wishes of the directors would need the approval of the Secretary of State. Backdoor nationalisation is not, therefore, likely to play a predominant part in the functioning of the N.E.B.

Much more important is likely to be its I.R.C. role of providing investment capital for companies and assisting the restructuring of an industry.[53] It has the power to make loans, guarantees and buy shares in companies[54] and can thus provide investment where private institutions are reluctant to do so either because of the risk or time-scale involved. Thus, the N.E.B. has taken financial shares in consortia bidding for foreign construction contracts. It is also financing a counter-cyclical scheme for the stockpiling of machine tools[55] and has increased the public shareholding in I.C.L. and Brown Boveri Kent.[56]

Whether this is the small beginning of a massive public investment in private industry will depend on private industry's willingness to invest and on the Government's willingness to make funds available to the N.E.B. If the funds of the N.E.B. are largely pre-empted by commitments to its subsidiaries such as British Leyland and Rolls-Royce there will not be much to spare for its dynamic role of regenerating British industry.

The N.E.B. has, therefore, been transformed from an instrument of nationalisation to an investment bank, development agency and holding company. All these functions were to some extent being performed by the Department of Industry before the creation of the N.E.B., though in a less active and entrepreneurial way. There is some overlap in the functions of the Department and the N.E.B.[57] but the main demarcation line is that the Department functions as a vet and the N.E.B. as a businessman. In practice this distinction will be somewhat blurred especially in respect of the N.E.B's function as a development agency and holding company but s.3 should at least prevent the blurring of

---

[52] Industry Act 1975, s.2(2)(*c*).
[53] Section 2(2)(a) and (b).
[54] Section 2(4). According to the guidelines the N.E.B. must charge commercial interest rates.
[55] 907 H.C. Deb., col. 1653 *et seq.* (March 18, 1976).
[56] 911 H.C. Deb., col. 934 (May 17, 1976). For a list of shareholdings, see 924 H.C. Deb., col.187, Written Answers (January 18, 1977).
[57] Especially in the case of schemes under s.8 of the Industry Act, 1972.

CHAPTER FIVE

MONITORING AND CONTROL BY GOVERNMENT DEPARTMENTS AND INDEPENDENT AGENCIES

So far we have been concerned with the different methods by which public money is provided for private industry and the controls over the provision of this money at the time that it is committed by the Government or an independent agency. We must now examine the monitoring of this expenditure after it has been committed first by the Government or independent agency and then by Parliament. The methods for providing aid to industry range from the acquisition of an undertaking to public purchasing policy. In between there are numerous powers to assist industry by taking shares, giving of grants, loans, guarantees, reliefs and allowances, providing aid through development contracts and launching aid as well as assistance in kind such as advisory services and research and industrial training facilities.[1] If monitoring of public expenditure were related to the type of assistance being provided, it would be helpful to examine the different categories of aid from this point of view. Methods of monitoring are, however, by no means related to the various kinds of aid and it is, therefore, preferable to examine the different mechanisms for controlling public expenditure.

APPOINTMENT OF CHAIRMAN

Where the Government or the N.E.B. own all the shares in an undertaking they have the power to select and remove the Chairman and directors. This is the position, for example, with regard to Cable and Wireless, Rolls-Royce (1971) Ltd., British Leyland Ltd. and Herbert Ltd.[2] and was the case with Beagle Aircraft Ltd.[3] The situation is similar where the Government owns the majority of shares. In the case of British Petroleum Ltd., in which the Government originally acquired

---

[1] For a comprehensive survey, see H.C. 347 (1971-2), vol. II, p.42 *et seq.*

[2] For list of Government directors, see 902 H.C. Deb., col. 62, Written Answers (December 8, 1975), and for transfer of shareholdings to the N.E.B., see 906 H.C. Deb., col. 387, Written Answers (February 27, 1976).

[3] H.C. 300-I (1970-1).

a majority of shares, the Government nominates only two directors but these have a power of veto over any resolution though the Government has pledged itself to use the veto only in defined circumstances[4] which will be further discussed below. The importance of the Government being the majority shareholder in order to be able to change the management was stressed both by the former Chairman of U.C.S.[5] and the former Chairman of Fairfields Ltd.[6]

There may, however, be special provisions for control by the Government over the chairman of a company even if the Government is a minority shareholder. Thus it was provided in the Computer Merger Scheme[7] under the Industrial Expansion Act 1968 that, so long as the Minister owned 5 per cent of the ordinary shares of I.C.L., he had to be consulted before the appointment or removal from office of the Chairman and Chief Executive.

The formal powers to select and/or change the Chairman of the company are only the tip of the iceberg. On numerous occasions the Government or an independent agency which has been asked for assistance by a firm has been able to bring about a change of management regardless of the size of its shareholding or in the absence of any equity stake in the company. In the case of **Beagle Aircraft Ltd.** the Government brought about the appointment of a new managing director before it acquired the undertaking.[8] Before the Government gave a further package of aid to I.C.L. a new chairman and managing director were appointed from outside.[9] Government nominees were appointed to the board of Alfred Herbert Ltd. before the Government acquired the equity[10] and one of these later replaced the acting chairman. The appointment of a new managing director and finance director to be approved by the Government was again one of the conditions upon which assistance was provided to Ferranti Ltd.[11] In the case of Rolls-Royce the Government brought about a change of chairman when it negotiated a £60 million package of aid shortly before the company went into liquidation.[12] Earlier, the I.R.C. had achieved management changes as a condition of receiving a £10 million loan as a first instalment.[13] Similarly, the S.I.B. made changes on the Board the precondi-

[4] H.C. 298 (1967-8), App. 1.
[5] H.C. 347 (1971-2), vol. II, Q.217.
[6] *Ibid.,* vol.III, Q.2247.
[7] S.I. 1968 No.990, cl.12, and see cl.10. See also the arrangements in the British Sugar Corporation, H.C.298 (1967-8), App. 1.
[8] H.C. 300-I (1970-1), Q.2450.
[9] *The Guardian,* July 5, 1973.
[10] 892 H.C. Deb., col. 242, Written Answers (May 19, 1975).
[11] 892 H.C. Deb., col. 457 (May 14, 1975).
[12] 806 H.C. Deb., col. 398 *et seq.* (November 11, 1970).
[13] Cmnd. 4860, para. 3.

tion for further assistance to U.C.S.[14] It is clear that both the Government and independent agencies have brought pressure to bear on a company to change its management as an essential ingredient of an aid package regardless of whether they owned part of the equity.

APPOINTMENT OF DIRECTORS

The Government may be given power to nominate directors in the articles of association of the company. This is the position in the case of B.P. Ltd. This is also the case with regard to I.C.L. where the Minister is given power to nominate one director so long as he holds 5 per cent of the shares.[15] Most legislation empowering the granting of assistance provides that the body giving aid may attach such conditions as it thinks fit. This power may be used to make the giving of aid conditional on the nomination of a director. This was done by the Shipbuilding Industry Board in the case of U.C.S.[16] The I.R.C. also used this power and had nominee directors in eight companies.[17] Lord Beeching was the nominee of the I.R.C. on the board of Rolls-Royce.[18] In the case of Ferranti Ltd.,[19] the Meriden co-operative[20] and Chrysler UK Ltd.,[21] the right to nominate one or more directors was one of the conditions on which assistance was granted under the Industry Act 1972.

It has been the exception rather than the rule to appoint Government directors where assistance is given under the Industry Act.[22] The exceptions will be cases where the Government is taking an equity stake or providing large sums of money[23] but the Meriden co-operative falls under neither category though it was an exceptionally controversial case. One of the reasons for exercising this power sparingly is the difficulty of finding suitable people.[24] Civil servants will not necessarily have the expertise of running a business whilst outside businessmen will not have the feel of the Department unless they have had experience of working in a Government Department, as is the case in the Industrial Development Unit. But the real problem with regard to the appointment of Government directors relates to their functions which raise issues of divided loyalties.

[14] H.C. 397 (1968-9), p.250, para. 12.
[15] Cmnd. 3660, para. 14(b).
[16] H.C. 397 (1968-9), Q.1448.
[17] H.C. 286 (1968-9), p.15.
[18] Cmnd. 4860, para. 3.
[19] 892 H.C. Deb., col. 457 (May 14, 1975).
[20] 878 H.C. Deb., col. 13, Written Answers (July 29, 1974). No director has yet been appointed
— H.C. 584 (1975-6), Q. 2698.
[21] 902 H.C. Deb., col. 1168 (December 16, 1975), and H.C. 104-i (1975-6), p. 16, cl.8(1).
[22] H.C. 303 (1974), Q. 133, p.26.
[23] *Ibid.,* Q. 148, p. 29, and H.C. 374 (1974-5), Q. 470.
[24] *Ibid.,* Q. 487, *et seq.*

Government directors may have special functions conferred on them in relation to the company.[25] An example of this is the veto power of the two directors appointed by the Government to B.P. Ltd. However, this power, which has never been used, is in fact vested in the Government and the directors act as channels of information rather than decision-makers.[26] The Government in their observations on the Expenditure Committee's report on 'Public Money in the Private Sector' promised 'to continue to ensure that any special duties of a Government director in a particular case are carefully defined with a view to avoiding any misunderstanding or conflict of interest.' [27]

It is the potential conflict of interest between the director's duties to the Government and the company which raises the problem. Both the former managing director of the I.R.C. and the Permanent Secretary to the Treasury drew attention to the difficulties of reconciling these conflicting interests.[28] The point was made very forcibly by a T.U.C. witness who said, 'I think it is the case at the moment that you cannot appoint a public director who is looking after the public interest; he has still to look after the interest of the shareholders.'[29] The same point was made by a Government spokesman in the House of Lords during the passage of the Industrial Expansion Bill.[30]

The way in which such directors have been regarded by both Government and industry sheds some light on how this conflict of interests is resolved. A Conservative minister, Sir John Eden, when giving evidence to the Science and Technology Committee about I.C.L., said that the Government do not have any special relationship via a Government nominated director.[31] Similarly, Mr. Benn, when giving evidence about U.C.S., said: 'It has never been our objective that we should deal with the company through Government directors. Government directors are directors of the company. They have special responsibilities which are understood. I think it would completely undermine the authority of the Chairman if he felt that one member of the Board was dealing with the Government or the S.I.B. without his being consulted.'[32] The former Chairman of U.C.S. endorsed this attitude to the Government director. When asked by the Expenditure Committee whether he was regarded as a spy by the Board, Mr. Hepper firmly denied this and answered, 'We regarded him as a colleague who had spe-

---

[25] See Daintith in Friedmann & Garner, *op. cit.,* p.67, n.56.
[26] *Ibid.,* p. 66-7.
[27] Cmnd. 5186, p.4.
[28] H.C. 347 (1971-2), vol. III, Qs. 1831 and 2525.
[29] *Ibid.,* vol. II, Q. 1595.
[30] 292 H.L., Deb., col. 424 (May 16, 1968).
[31] H.C. 621-II (1970-1), Q. 647.
[32] H.C. 397 (1968-9), Q. 1448.

cial responsibility for reporting our affairs independently to our major shareholder.'[33] The same view of such directors' functions was taken by the civil servants of the Department when giving evidence to the Public Accounts Committee. The Secretary (Industry) saw their function as keeping an eye on the Government's interest and being available to give advice[34] but stressed that they must not be put in a position where they were suspected of being Government spies as they are directors under the Companies Acts.[35] He also made the point that in most cases the necessary information could be obtained from contacts with the company and through monitoring activities without appointing Government directors.

The weakness of the non-executive director's position was pointed out by Mr. Morrow, the Managing Director of Rolls-Royce (1971) Ltd., in evidence to the Expenditure Committee in their inquiry into 'Public Money in the Private Sector.'[36] Lord Beeching reinforced the same point when he contrasted his position as I.R.C. director on the board of Rolls-Royce with the normal non-executive director.[37] He was provided with any information for which he asked and took a much more active role than is usual for a non-executive director who would not have sufficient knowledge. Other witnesses before the Committee were enthusiastic about the appointment of non-executive directors from outside the company so as to bring in some fresh experience[38] but they were saying this in the general context of control by shareholders over their directors rather than as a mechanism for Government control over public money invested in the company. Certainly no great enthusiasm was expressed about the appointment of two Government directors to Chrysler UK Ltd. during the debates on the financial assistance to that company.[39] Some M.Ps wondered what their functions would be and hoped that they would be more effective than Government nominees had been in the past. One M.P. criticised the two B.P. directors for not taking any notice of Mr. Heath's energy policy as members of a Board which took into account purely commercial considerations. Another M.P. thought that two Tibetan monks might have been equally effective on the Board.[40] Similarly, the T.U.C., when giving evidence to the Expenditure Committee, criticised Government nominees as being merely passive

[33] H.C. 347 (1971-2), vol.III, Qs. 2116 and 2118.
[34] H.C. 303 (1974), Qs. 148 and 149, p.29.
[35] H.C.374 (1974-5), Q. 489.
[36] H.C. 347 (1971-2), vol. III, Qs. 2709 and 2710.
[37] *Ibid.,* Q. 1922 *et seq.*
[38] *Ibid.,* Qs. 1830 and 2012.
[39] 902 H.C. Deb., col. 1256 (December 16, 1975), and *ibid.,* col. 1551 (December 17, 1975).
[40] Industry Bill, Standing Committee E, March 25, 1975, col. 484.

spectators rather than active managers.[41]

The question of management will be further discussed below but it is clear that nominee directors have only a very limited role to play as channels of communication between the Government and the company. It has been stressed repeatedly by Ministers and confirmed by industry that the Chairman is the main channel of communication between the Government and the company. This was stressed by Sir John Eden in relation to I.C.L. and Mr. Benn with regard to U.C.S. It was confirmed by the Government in their observations on the Expenditure Committee's report and it was bitterly regretted by both the former chairmen of U.C.S.[42] and Fairfields Ltd.[43] that this contact had not been closer. In the memorandum which established the relationship between Rolls-Royce (1971) Ltd. and the Government it was expressly stated that 'The Chairman will at all times have access to the responsible Minister to discuss any matters he or the Board wishes to raise with the Government'[44] and this right remains open since the transfer to the N.E.B. provided the N.E.B. is consulted beforehand.[45]

But the Chairman is by no means the only channel of communication between the Government and a company it is assisting financially. The provision of information to the Government, its timing and monitoring have all given rise to great problems whose solution is crucial to enabling the Government to exercise control over public money.

MONITORING

The lack of information at the right time played a part in several of the rescue operations in which the Government has been involved. One of the main problems in these cases was the lack of adequate accounting systems within the firm so that the management itself was not in possession of the necessary information. The Department told the Expenditure Committee that this was the situation in the case of U.C.S.[46] and the former chairman of Rolls-Royce himself told the Committee that their accounting system was not satisfactory for the purposes of monitoring contracts.[47] This was reiterated by the former chairman of the I.R.C. who said that the firm did not know what was happening.[48] He laid some of the blame for this on the Government who over the years

---

[41] H.C. 347, vol. II (1971-2), Q. 1595. The Report of the Expenditure Committee also did not put great faith in the appointment of Government directors, H.C. 347 (1971-2), para. 264.
[42] *Ibid.*, Qs.2113, 2142 and 2180.
[43] *Ibid.*, Q.2276.
[44] 874 H.C. Deb., col. 389 *et seq.*, Written Answers (June 4, 1974).
[45] Memorandum of Understanding about the Relationship between the N.E.B. and RR71.
[46] H.C. 347 (1971-2), vol.III, Qs. 2309 and 3010.
[47] *Ibid.*, Q. 2063.
[48] *Ibid.*, vol.II, Q.1204, and vol.III, Q.1742.

had misgivings about the financial control system but did nothing to strengthen it.[49] When Mr. Morrow as deputy chairman of Rolls-Royce (1971) Ltd. joined the board he showed that the forecasts were over-optimistic and did not make sufficient allowance for contingencies.[50]

In each of these cases, when the final crisis came, the Government was taken by surprise because the firm itself was in the dark until the last moment.[51] In the case of U.C.S. the Government received a great deal of detailed information but it was still not adequate[52] and it was late.[53] In the case of Rolls-Royce, though the Government monitored the RB211 project more closely than is usual in the case of launching aid[54] and a review by Cooper Bros. was in progress, there was no warning of the final crisis.

The Government was similarly taken by surprise in the case of Beagle Aircraft Ltd.,[55] a company which in contradistinction to U.C.S. and Rolls-Royce was at the time of its liquidation wholly owned by the Government. After acquisition, the Government relaxed some of the control which it had exercised in the period before transfer when it had in principle agreed to acquire the assets. Instead of quarterly progress meetings to discuss and approve development plans, there were to be six-monthly meetings for a general review of the company's affairs. The first of these was postponed and no detailed programme was then available. When this was finally presented two months later it became apparent that liquidation was the only alternative to a much larger investment by the Government. The Ministry could not say whether they would have been forewarned about this crisis earlier if they had not relaxed control after acquisition but the Public Accounts Committee thought that either the Ministry could not have paid sufficient attention to the information they had which should have given them earlier warning of the position of the company, or that contacts had not been close enough.

Many lessons have been learnt from these cases and very detailed monitoring arrangements have been evolved by the Department. In the case of Govan Shipbuilders, which is the successor of U.C.S., the Department received detailed financial information including monthly cash flow statements; monthly, quarterly and six-monthly

---

[49] *Ibid.*, Q.1788.
[50] *Ibid.*, Q.2688.
[51] *Ibid.*, Q.2309 — U.C.S. H.C. 347 (1971-2), para.71 — Rolls-Royce Ltd.
[52] *Ibid.*, Q.2314.
[53] *Ibid.*, Q.3011.
[54] H.C. 447 (1971-2), para. 22.
[55] See H.C. 300-I (1970-71), para. 49 *et seq.*

profit and loss statements; annual report and accounts; and a corporate plan revised annually. A monthly schedule for each yard showing the steelwork performance and shipbuilding programme was received together with copies of the minutes of board meetings. The Managing Director reported separately each month, commenting on the order book position, capital spending, industrial relations and general financial matters.[56] There were also regular meetings both at the company premises and in the Department at least monthly and at higher levels less frequently.[57] The capital development programme for reconstruction of the yards was supervised by the company's management consultants whose reports were available to the Department. The Department were opposed to appointing a firm of management consultants from outside to undertake the monitoring of the firm as they had established a close working relationship with the company and understood their problems.[58] They had had early warning through a revised corporate plan which they requested, that viability would not be achieved within the five years originally predicted and that further assistance would be necessary.[59] This is in marked contrast to the earlier crisis when the Department was taken by surprise. After nationalisation, monitoring will be the responsibility of British Shipbuilders of which Govan will be a subsidiary.[60]

So far as investment grants and now regional development grants are concerned, the object of monitoring is to ensure that the grant is used for the purpose for which it was provided. This involves inspection of the premises to ensure that the asset is there and that the premises have not ceased to qualify.[61] In the case of construction plant this could be used anywhere within the development area. There have undoubtedly been problems where plant has been moved out of development areas which has not been detected.[62]

It is more difficult to monitor selective assistance because it is easier to ensure that the money is used for the purposes provided than to assess whether the money has achieved its purpose, e.g. by providing

[56] 886 H.C. Deb., col. 490, Written Answers (February 20, 1975).
[57] H.C. 303 (1974), Qs. 139 and 140, p.26.
[58] H.C. 374 (1974-5), Q.570.
[59] *Ibid.*, Qs. 553 and 565.
[60] Aircraft and Shipbuilding Industries Bill, Standing Committee D, February 17, 1976, col. 955 *et seq.* Pending nationalisation a holding company has been established for the publicly-owned shareholdings in shipbuilding companies which will undertake functions of management and monitoring on behalf of the Department — 925 H.C. Deb., col.489, Written Answers (February 7, 1977).
[61] H.C. 303 (1974), Q.71, p.12 *et seq.*
[62] 894 H.C. Deb., cols. 502 and 552 (June 25, 1975).

new employment.[63] Monitoring is concerned with both these objectives as well as safeguarding the Government's investment.[64]

The Government try as far as possible to rely for these purposes on information which the company uses for its own management purposes. They must, therefore, assure themselves at the outset that these management information systems can provide the necessary information which, as we have seen, is not always the case. The contractual documents between the Government and the firm will contain the power to obtain the required information. This will vary according to the amount of assistance and the degree of risk involved. In the case of interest relief grants, which account for the great majority of assistance under s.7 of the Industry Act 1972, it is merely a matter of checking that the stipulated conditions have been met before payment is made as the loan itself comes from commercial sources.[65] Where there is a loan which is not large and no great risk, the minimum requirement for information is the provision of historical accounts, i.e. audited annual accounts and half-yearly management accounts. However, as the stake or the risk increases the Department may require a corporate plan setting out the company's objectives, policy options and strategy, an annual operating plan with physical targets, an annual budget and quarterly or monthly reports comparing progress with targets.[66]

In order to monitor this information the Department has appointed monitoring officers[67] who go to special training courses selected for this purpose.[68] A monitoring officer has been allocated to each project though he will of course deal with a number of cases. In the case of the Kirkby co-operative where there was a grant not a loan, a senior monitoring officer has been appointed to ensure that the money is used for the purposes for which it was provided.[69] If the monitoring officer suspects trouble, particularly if the appointment of a receiver is contemplated, he must go to the regional industrial director who would refer to the Industrial Development Unit in important cases.[70] The Advisory Boards would also be available to give advice in such cases.

---

[63] H.C. 303 (1974), Q.148, p.27.
[64] *Ibid.*, App. 2.
[65] *Ibid.*, Q.150, p.28, and H.C. 374 (1974-5), Q.470.
[66] For specimen monitoring plans, see H.C. 374 (1974-5), App. IV.
[67] 58 staff were engaged on monitoring work throughout Great Britain in January, 1975, H.C.617-I (1974-5), p.6.
[68] H.C. 374 (1974-5), Q.470.
[69] *Ibid.*, Q.471. In the case of the Scottish Daily News, another co-operative which was given a loan, the position was monitored weekly (H.C. 78 (1975-6), para.27).
[70] H.C. 303 (1974), Q.136, p.26.

The Department may also use outside consultants to assist in monitoring. This was done in the case of the initial guarantees for Ferranti's[71] and Coopers and Lybrand have been appointed to advise the Department on monitoring the assistance to Chrysler.[72]

In the case of Chrysler, the agreement with the Secretary of State[73] provides for the keeping of proper accounting records which must be open to inspection by the Secretary of State at all reasonable times and the furnishing of quarterly accounts, audited balance sheet and any financial and other information reasonably required by him as to the activities, affairs, plans and prospects of Chrysler U.K. Ltd. There are monthly monitoring meetings between the Department and the company. Most important for the purposes of monitoring the investment of public money are the conditions contained in the agreement upon which payments in respect of the £55 million loan depend. In particular clause 5(vii) provides that prior to each advance Chrysler must certify 'that in its opinion the progress being made towards the objectives of the Stoke Linwood and Truck Plan and the C6 Programme is sufficient to warrant the continuation of the capital expenditure envisaged by those plans; and in giving such a certificate C.U.K. shall have regard particularly to the question of whether satisfactory agreements between the C.U.K. Group and representatives of its workforce have been concluded, or whether there is a reasonable prospect that such agreements will be concluded within a reasonable time concerning numbers to be employed, productivity and related matters, and whether any such agreements which have been concluded are being satisfactorily implemented.' This condition did not satisfy the Advisory Board who wanted binding arrangements with the workforce concerning manning levels, productivity and other key factors determining competitiveness as well as giving the Government power to curtail or vary its commitment in the light of events.[74]

This is the position in the case of British Leyland where after the initial injection of £200 million new equity capital, loans up to £500 million will be phased over three years and will be released in the light of the contribution being made to improvements in performance by

---

[71] H.C. 374 (1974-5), Q.470.

[72] 904 H.C. Deb., col.93, Written Answers (January 26, 1976).

[73] H.C. 104-i (1975-6), p.9 *et seq.*

[74] *Ibid.,* p.4. In the case of Govan Shipbuilders Ltd. continued support was made conditional on the Secretary of State's continuing to be satisfied with the company's progress towards its productivity targets as indicated in the monitoring information, — 897 H.C. Deb., col. 506, Written Answers (August 7, 1975). The Public Accounts Committee was concerned that in practice the commitment would become open-ended, see H.C. 556 (1975-6), para.30.

better industrial relations and higher productivity.[75] The Expenditure Committee was sceptical about the practical possibility of withholding a tranche as a sanction.[76] The Government in its reply to this report denied that this was a sanction which could not be used. That this is not an empty threat was shown in December, 1975 when the investment programme was temporarily halted by the company with the approval of Lord Ryder, the chairman of the National Enterprise Board, because it had failed to meet its financial targets.[77] As a subsidiary of the N.E.B., British Leyland's long-term and annual operating plans have to be agreed with the N.E.B. and discussed with the Government. Progress against the plan is monitored throughout the year by the N.E.B., who report periodically to the Government.[78] The N.E.B. has to ensure that ways of measuring progress and identifying targets of achievement are discussed between the company and the unions and agreed with the Government and these will provide the basis on which further tranches of money will be released. This decision will be one of major policy to be taken by Ministers collectively.[79]

Rolls-Royce (1971) Ltd. will also now be monitored as a subsidiary by the N.E.B. The Memorandum of Understanding which embodies the concordat reached between these two bodies lays down that RR71's long-range and annual plans will be subject to agreement by the N.E.B. and that RR71 will supply the N.E.B. with such information as to enable the N.E.B. to monitor the performance of the company. There were similar provisions in the earlier memorandum which established the relationship between RR71 and the Government.[80] Under this the company agreed with the Government to provide (1) a long-term corporate plan looking ten to fifteen years ahead. (2) a five-year forecast, (3) annual budgets and (4) regular monthly reports comparing performance with budgets.[81] These monthly reports were stopped for a time because the Chairman of Rolls-Royce had no confidence in them and outside consultants were commissioned to improve the information services within the company. New internal management control systems were installed in the company after discussion

---

[75] 890 H.C. Deb., col. 1746 (April 24, 1975), and see Ryder Report, H.C. 342 (1974-5), Chap. 15.23. The Opposition spokesman's comment on these checks was that they should apply not only after but before the injection of over £200 million equity capital — 892 H.C. Deb., col. 1452 (May 21, 1975).

[76] H.C. 617 (1974-5), para. 257 *et seq.*

[77] *The Guardian,* December 10, 1975.

[78] Cmnd. 6377, p.10 *et seq.*, and H.C. 104-xix (1975-6), Q.3775 *et seq.*

[79] H.C. 617-II (1974-5), Q.2769, H.C. 104-xxii (1975-6), Q.4307 *et seq.*, and 916 H.C. Deb., col.1601 (August 3, 1976) for release of first tranche.

[80] 874 H.C. Deb., col. 389, Written Answers (June 4, 1974).

[81] H.C. 303 (1974), para. 23 *et seq.*

with the Department.[82] The company formulated a general strategy within which it submitted broad financial forecasts for the next five years on December 9, 1975.[83] The problem was how to reconcile RR71's relationships with the Government and the N.E.B. To solve this conflict the Memorandum of Understanding with the N.E.B. provides that, 'The N.E.B. will however be accompanied by representatives of RR71 at major discussions with Government of the plans of RR71 and will invite the RR71 representatives to explain the plans to the Government at those discussions. It will also be open to the chairman of RR71 at any time to seek a meeting with a Minister, provided that the chairman of the N.E.B. is consulted beforehand and has the opportunity to attend if he wishes.'[84] The solution to the conflict thus lay in granting RR71 equality of access to the Government with the N.E.B.

The Memorandum further provides that RR71 will maintain its dealings with Government Departments on day-to-day matters, including dealings with the Department of Industry in its role as sponsor Department for the aero-engine industry and dealings with the Ministry of Defence (Procurement Executive) on all matters for which it is responsible. This would seem to show that the monitoring of the RB211 engine will continue to be the responsibility of the Procurement Executive.[85] For this purpose the Ministry have appointed a project team led by a Project Director who has the assistance of specialist branches in assessing the technical and cost information submitted by the company. The Government have access to all information produced by the company about the project and may attend relevant company meetings. The company is required to follow agreed costed technical programmes and to seek prior approval for changes to them. Progress review meetings are held monthly with senior representatives of the company and the project team produces two-monthly technical and cost reports. Even this strict system of monitoring did not give adequate warning of cost increases in the case of the M45H engine but this seems to have been due to special circumstances and defects in the company's appraisal and reporting procedures which, as we have seen, were later improved.[86]

Though it was said in evidence to the Public Accounts Committee

[82] H.C. 502 (1974-5), Q.2102 *et seq.*, and H.C. 334 (1975-6), Q.709 *et seq.*
[83] 902 H.C. Deb., col. 778, Written Answers (December 18, 1975).
[84] Para. 13.
[85] H.C. 303 (1974), para. 27 *et seq.*
[86] H.C. 78 (1975-6), para. 35 *et seq.* Comptroller and Auditor General's Report on the Appropriation Accounts 1974-5, and H.C. 334 (1975-6), para. 54 *et seq.* — Public Accounts Committee Report.

that the RB211 was being handled on the lines of a military project,[87] the monitoring of Concorde was similarly close[88] which did not prevent it being criticised by the Public Accounts Committee, though they came to the conclusion that major savings would not have been possible within the constraints imposed by the nature of the project, i.e. once the decision had been taken to proceed in one stage with a speculative project of advanced technology.[89] It was partly the duplication of technical and financial experts and the detailed control which monitoring entailed which led the Plowden Committee to recommend that the Government should take a shareholding in the airframe companies to enable it to relax these controls.[90] The same point was made by the Secretary of State as one of the reasons for nationalisation on the Second reading of the Aircraft and Shipbuilding Industry Bill.[91] He argued that nationalisation would involve strategic control rather than detailed monitoring of individual projects. The Opposition spokesman was very sceptical of this claim[92] and the nationalisation of Rolls-Royce has certainly not led to a reduction in the monitoring of projects. It was a former Minister of Aviation, Mr. Julian Amery, who put forward the mirror image of the Secretary of State's argument against nationalisation. He said that the Government had the best of both worlds: 'They have control of the industry as customers and they have the advantages of the private enterprise system in that they are not responsible for its management and direction.'[93]

This distinction between monitoring and management has been constantly stressed by the Department. The Permanent Secretary when making his classic statement about monitoring to the Public Accounts Committee stressed that, 'all these arrangements must not be such as to remove the prime responsibility and main focus of initiative from the board of the company. That may sometimes be quite a difficult balance to hold, but it is very important that it should be held.'[94] How difficult it may be to draw this dividing line was illustrated by the evidence of his successor to later Public Accounts Committees who asked what would happen if the Department disagrees with the company's plans or the information obtained through monitoring signals danger. He replied that the Department would discuss with the company changes of plan, if necessary, and what steps to take but added, 'I

[87] H.C. 447 (1971-2), Q.1904.
[88] *Ibid.*, Q.1907.
[89] H.C. 335 (1972-3), para. 63.
[90] Cmnd. 2853 (1965), Chap. 37.
[91] 901 H.C. Deb., col. 1451 (December 2, 1975).
[92] *Ibid.*, col. 1464.
[93] *Ibid.*, col. 1484.
[94] H.C. 447 (1971-2), Q.1548.

think the dividing line would be quite a difficult one to draw, where we began to insist that our judgment was right and the company's judgment was wrong.'[95]

So far we have considered control through monitoring techniques but there are other methods of control which the Government may have which will now be considered and in this context it is very relevant to bear in mind the statement with which Mr. Amery prefaced the remarks just quoted, 'The issue is not one of ownership but one of control.' An examination of the interrelationship of these concepts will reveal how far control is dependent on ownership and the extent to which ownership imports control.

CONTROL AND OWNERSHIP

The relationship between the Government and a company limited under the Companies Act which is fully owned by the Government is well illustrated by Beagle Aircraft Ltd. As we saw, the Government after the acquisition of the company modified its relationship so as to cut down the frequency of monitoring.[96] The policy of the Government was that the company should operate as a normal commercial company which should be judged by normal commercial standards. The Chairman was given a broad policy remit which required him to ensure that the Board formulated policies and programmes for the commercial success of the company and he had to obtain the approval of the Minister for (a) incurring any substantial expenditure on capital account; (b) any activity of the company not essential to the business of developing, producing and selling light aircraft; (c) the disposal of any substantial part of the company's assets; and (d) the association of the company with foreign companies or foreign-controlled companies in the United Kingdom.[97] Within this broad policy remit the Board were responsible for the day-to-day management of the company and the Department were firmly convinced that, having set up the company, they should not be continually breathing down its neck. The relationship with the company was, therefore, very much at arm's length.

Though, as we saw above, the Government learnt a lesson from Beagle's collapse so far as monitoring of information is concerned, the relationship between the Government and fully-owned companies established later was defined in a way very similar to Beagle's. The memorandum establishing the relationship between Rolls-Royce

[95] H.C. 303 (1974), Q.129, p.25, and H.C.374 (1974-5), Q.494-5.
[96] See generally on Beagle Aircraft Ltd., H.C. 300-I (1970-1), para.49 *et seq.*
[97] *Ibid.*, Q.2657.

(1971) Ltd. and the Government stated: 'It is the wish of both parties that the board of the company should as far as possible operate as though it were the board of a privately-owned company established under the Companies Acts; and it is not the Government's intention, as sole shareholder, to concern themselves with the day-to-day running of the company or to diminish in any way the responsibility of the board for the conduct of the company's affairs. The Government will expect the company to act commercially and to earn a commercial return on its capital employed.'[98]

It was the fear of losing this independence when Rolls-Royce was transferred to the N.E.B. which led to the drawing up of the Memorandum of Understanding between RR71 and the N.E.B. This reaffirmed that RR71 should operate as far as possible like a private company on a normal commercial basis and stated that the N.E.B. would not intervene in day-to-day management. But, as we have seen, RR71's plans will now be subject to agreement with the N.E.B. whose approval is also necessary for capital expenditure projects of £5 million and over. Their approval must also be sought for acquisitions of share capital of a company above a certain level or the disposal of shares. RR71's social obligations to locate expansion in development areas and to further worker participation are also spelt out as well as the need to ensure that the Government's counter-inflation policy is observed in the negotiation of pay settlements.[99] A similar provision in the earlier memorandum between the Government and RR71 was put to the test when RR71 broke the earlier Social Contract negotiated with the T.U.C. and earned itself a stern rebuke from Mr. Foot, the Employment Secretary, with a veiled threat that financial aid could be withdrawn but without any further action.[100]

Action was, however, taken by the Government a few months earlier when the Government requested the company to terminate its contracts with Chile for the maintenance of aircraft engines and supply of parts.[101] In answer to a supplementary question whether Rolls-Royce would be paid compensation for this cancellation Mr. Benn replied with a curt 'No'.[102] This is an illustration of intervention in the affairs of a publicly-owned company for political reasons which has been so much a feature of the relationship between the nationalised industries and the Minister. Further instances are foreshadowed in the Memorandum of Understanding with the N.E.B. which provides for

[98] 874 H.C. Deb., col. 389, Written Answers (June 4, 1974).
[99] As set out in the White Paper 'The Attack on Inflation,' Cmnd.6151.
[100] 881 H.C. Deb., col. 490, Written Answers (November 21, 1974).
[101] 874 H.C. Deb., col. 186 (May 21, 1974).
[102] *Ibid.*, col. 391, Written Answers (June 4, 1974).

advance warning to the N.E.B. and the Secretary of State of any decisions which have major Parliamentary implications.[103] The same problem will arise with regard to other companies whose shares are wholly-
owned by the N.E.B. The issue was raised by Lord Stokes in relation
to British Leyland when giving evidence to the Expenditure Committee[104] and Mr. Biffen asked in a debate on assistance to Alfred Herbert
Ltd. whether the firm's interests in South Africa would be affected by
the Government's acquisition of the company's shares.[105]

The reverse side of this coin, namely the damage which political
interference in the affairs of a wholly-owned company operating
abroad can do to its image of independence and, therefore, its business
activities, was strongly relied on by the Government in the case of
Cable & Wireless Ltd. when objecting to its inclusion in the terms of
reference of the Select Committee on Nationalised Industries.[106] The
Government owns all the shares of this company and appoints the
directors. The company must obtain the approval of the Treasury for
major capital expenditure and submits five-year plans for capital
expenditure to the Treasury for approval. It raises all its capital from
its own resources and declares a dividend. The losses made by one of
its subsidiary companies gave rise to criticism by Social Audit, a group
financed partly by the Consumers' Association, who called for greater
public accountability of the company.[107] This led to a detailed examination by the Department of Industry which brought about changes in
the form of the accounts and arrangements to improve the regular
flow of information from the company to the Department.[108] It was
later announced that the Government had relaxed restrictions on the
company's freedom to provide telecommunications 'private systems'
subject to consultation with the Government.[109] This episode illustrates that, in spite of the Government's policy of non-interference in
the running of the company, it was forced by public criticism to examine its affairs and keep them under closer review. The Government in
1969 also retracted its objection to including the company in the
Nationalised Industries Committee's terms of reference which in 1975-
6 made an inquiry into the firm.[110] The facade of independence of this
company has, therefore, been somewhat dented.

---

[103] Clause 12.
[104] H.C. 617-I (1974-5) Q.300 seq. But he also acknowledged that the problem already existed for
British Leyland before any Government investment.
[105] 901 H.C. Deb. col. 1626 (December 2, 1975).
[106] See H.C. 298 (1967-8), para. 72 *et seq.* and Q.195 *et seq.*
[107] 'The Guardian' December 2, 1974. This was followed by a Question by Mr. Stanley, 882 H.C.
Deb. col. 621, Written Answers (December 5, 1974).
[108] 886 H.C. Deb., col. 201, Written Answers (February 13, 1975).
[109] 899 H.C. Deb., col. 404, Written Answers (November 10, 1975).
[110] H.C. 472 (1975-6).

Similar issues arise in connection with the relationship between the Government and British Petroleum Ltd. The Government acquired a controlling interest in this company in 1914 which was reduced to 48 per cent in 1966 when more shares were issued. When 20 per cent of B.P. shares owned by the Burmah Oil Co. were transferred to the Bank of England,[111] the Government virtually owned 70 per cent. of B.P. but it gave an undertaking to the City Take-over Panel that this would not change its existing relationship with the firm and that it would not exercise a greater proportionate voting power in relation to other shareholders than it could have exercised hitherto.[112] Under the existing position the Government can exercise control through the right to nominate two directors who have a right of veto over any resolution, subject to a right of appeal by other directors to the Treasury and Admiralty. The veto has never been used and the Government advised the company that it would only be used in regard to certain matters of general policy such as defence and foreign affairs.[113] Successive Governments have accepted that they would not for other reasons interfere in the commercial activities of the company. Though there is contact with the Treasury when the dividend is about to be declared and capital issues are under consideration, the relationship with the Government is in essence the same as that of any other oil company. It was for this reason and because it might lead to misunderstanding abroad about the commercial independence of the company that the Minister objected to the inclusion of the company in the Nationalised Industries Committee's terms of reference.[114] Again, the company was not used as an instrument for implementing the Government's policy on oil because 90 per cent of its operations were overseas and, according to one expert witness before the Nationalised Industries Committee investigating the exploitation of North Sea Oil and Gas, the use of B.P. for this purpose by the Government would have had serious repercussions in relation to other oil companies.

Nevertheless, when controversial issues have arisen in relation to B.P. and particularly since the exploration of North Sea Oil, the Government has been under pressure to intervene in the affairs of the company. There was strong criticism of the company's actions during the Arab oil embargo when it was accused of not acting in the national interest. It is, therefore, probably not fortuitous that B.P. was the first major oil company not in financial difficulties to agree to a majority

---

[111] 884 H.C. Deb., col. 448 (January 15, 1975).
[112] 887 H.C. Deb. col. 314 (February 25, 1975).
[113] H.C. 298 (1967-8) para. 64 *et seq.* and Q.102 *et seq.* H.C.345 (1974-5) paras. 72 *et seq.* and Q.575 *et seq.*
[114] See also H.C. 345 (1974-5) Q.583.

stake by the Government in its North Sea oilfields.[115] However, the Government was criticised for allowing an American company rather than B.P. to become the operator of the Ninian Oilfield.[116] The involvement of B.P. in payments to Italian politicians was also very embarrassing for the Government.[117] In the highly politically charged atmosphere surrounding oil it will probably become increasingly difficult for the Government to maintain its arm's length relationship with B.P. particularly if it retains a majority stake.

Another company in which the Government has a majority stake and with which it has an arm's length relationship is Short Bros. and Harland Ltd., the aircraft company situated in Belfast.[118] The directive given to the Chairman and Directors is similar to that in the case of Beagle Aircraft and includes the obtaining of the Minister's approval before entering on a course of action which might raise controversial public issues.[119] It must have regard to general Government policy but is expected to function as a normal commercial company. The Government has stated that the company is judged by the same criteria as other suppliers when undertaking Government contracts[120] and Mr. Benn, in evidence to the Select Committee on Nationalised Industries, stressed that the relationship with the company was similar to that with a private aircraft company such as B.A.C. When asked about the special employment considerations in Northern Ireland he equated them with the similar position of firms in the development areas in which the Government had no stake. These are presumably the political considerations which the Plowden committee said had influenced the Government's attitude to Short's.[121] The basic point that the Minister was making was that the links between Government and private industry, particularly the aircraft industry, were becoming closer and that there was, therefore, less difference between publicly- and privately-owned firms. Mr. Benn's evidence highlights the fact that ownership of shares is not crucial to the relationship between the Government and the company which is confirmed by the Plowden Committee's findings of the detailed control exercised over the private aircraft companies. Here, therefore, it is not ownership which imports control but contract.

The same can be said of the relationship between the Government

---

[115] 899 H.C. Deb., col. 382, Written Answers (November 10, 1975) and 914 H.C. Deb., col. 237 Written Answers (July 1, 1976).

[116] 887 H.C. Deb., col.14 (February 24, 1975).

[117] 909 H.C. Deb., col. 1218 (April 13, 1976) and 911 H.C. Deb., col. 1213 (May 18, 1976).

[118] For restructuring of the company, see 919 H.C. Deb., col.932, Written Answers (November 22, 1976).

[119] H.C. 298 (1967-8), paras. 90, *et seq.*, and Q.132, *et seq.*

[120] 885 H.C. Deb., col. 628, Written Answers (February 6, 1975).

[121] Cmnd. 2853, p.85n.

and International Computers Ltd. (I.C.L.). The Government acquired a 10 per cent shareholding[122] under the Computer Merger Scheme made under the Industrial Expansion Act 1968.[123] So long as the Minister held not less than 5 per cent of the ordinary shares, his approval was necessary for any association by I.C.L. with foreign companies or any major change in the nature of its business or disposal of its assets. The Minister made it clear that he would not use his shareholding to interfere in the day-to-day management of the company.[124] This was well illustrated by the Government's disclaimer of responsibility for the sale of a computer to South Africa by I.C.L. for use in computerising the pass law system.[125]

The Government is not, however, merely a shareholder of I.C.L. As we have seen, it has provided grants towards research and development expenditure of I.C.L. in three packages totalling £53½ million. The first package of £13½ million contribution to R. & D. expenditure which was payable in four instalments was not only conditional upon yearly increases in R. & D. expenditure by I.C.L. and reports on future and past R. & D. expenditure coupled with access to the premises of the group by the Minister for the purpose of monitoring the R. & D. expenditure, but the agreement also provided that I.C.L. would give due weight to the views of the Minister in framing its R. & D. programme for this period.[126] The agreement then went on to declare that it was the intention of I.C.L. to 'go ahead with the development of a large computer system of such reasonable specification and cost as may be appropriate to meet orders that Her Majesty's Government intends to place for such a system and other expected demands at home and overseas' and 'pursue the development of a successor range to the 1900 Series and the System 4 range . . .' The £40 million 'launching aid' provided in 1972 and 1973 was for the development of a new 2900 Series range of computers of which it seems the Government is to be the first customer.[127] As we have seen, the Government also operates a purchasing policy of computers for Government use under which large computers are purchased from I.C.L. by single tender.[128] The company in its evidence to the Select Committee on Science and Technology denied that launching aid influenced the direction of its product strategy and claimed that the initiative came from the firm.[129]

---

[122] This stake has now been vested in and increased to 24 per cent by the N.E.B. — see 911 H.C. Deb., col. 934 (May 17, 1976).
[123] S.I. 1968 No.990.
[124] Cmnd. 3660, para. 5.
[125] 861 H.C. Deb., col. 50, Written Answers (October 16, 1973).
[126] S.I. 1968 No. 990, cl. 10 and 11.
[127] 894 H.C. Deb., col. 264, Written Answers (June 27, 1975) and H.C. 199-i (1974), Q.56.
[128] 812 H.C. Deb., col. 419, Written Answers (March 2, 1971).
[129] H.C. 97-I (1972-3), Q.165.

The Committee, however, were fearful of the dangers inherent in the Government's policy. 'In a situation where support is directed specifically towards one company with frequent contacts with Departments, it is only too easy for Ministers and civil servants to become involved in policy making or even in the company's day-to-day management. This can threaten the freedom of the management to act in the manner which they believe to be in the interests of the company.'[130] Thus, as in the case of the aircraft industry, it is launching aid and the Government's purchasing policy rather than ownership of equity which gives the Government power over the company's affairs.

CONCLUSION

One of the conclusions which may be drawn from the foregoing examination is that the extent of control over a company is not in direct proportion to the amount of equity owned by the Government. Though ownership of all the shares enables the Government or N.E.B. to appoint and remove the Chairman and all the directors, there may be specific powers over the Chairman even with a minority stake and where assistance is under consideration the Government or independent agency may be able to exert pressures without acquiring any stake in the company. The power to appoint directors may exist quite apart from the acquisition of any equity and they have in any case a limited role to play.

The amount of information required by the Government to enable it to monitor assistance provided under the Industry Acts is related to the magnitude of the assistance and the risk involved rather than the size of the equity stake held by the Government. In the case of Beagle Aircraft Ltd. the Government cut down the frequency of its monitoring after it had acquired the company. This has not been true in the case of monitoring projects for which the Government provides launching aid such as the RB211 where monitoring was tightened after the acquisition of Rolls-Royce (1971) Ltd. But as is illustrated by Concorde the monitoring of launching aid in the case of aircraft projects is related to the extent to which the Department bears the risk of the project not to the stake the Government has in the company concerned.

It was to reverse this state of affairs, to substitute strategic for detailed controls, that the Plowden Committee recommended that the Government should take a shareholding in the aircraft companies. The nationalisation of Rolls-Royce, as we have seen, did not have this effect; whether the nationalisation of the aircraft industry will have the

---

[130] H.C. 309 (1972-3), para. 56.

intended result remains to be seen. Both forms of nationalisation are intended to give the Minister strategic control but to leave the public corporation or firm free in matters of day-to-day management. Though they have this aim in common, in practice they embody very different relationships with the Minister. This distinction was drawn by the then Secretary of State, Mr. Davies, when asked about his relationship with Govan Shipbuilders[131] and Mr. Benn in his evidence to the Nationalised Industries Committee also stressed the difference.[132] He was at pains to draw the analogy between his relationship with Government-owned companies and private industry rather than the nationalised industries. Though Mr. Davies rightly warned that it was difficult to generalise as each case is an individual one, the relationship with companies in which the Government holds all or the majority of shares does seem to be modelled on that with private industry.

The memorandum embodying the relationship between the Government and Rolls-Royce (1971) Ltd. as well as the later concordat between the N.E.B. and RR71 expressly declared that the company should operate as far as possible like a privately-owned company. The same instruction was contained in the directive to the Chairman and directors of Beagle Aircraft and Short's.[133] Cable and Wireless is regarded by the Government as a commercial concern and this is *a fortiori* true of B.P. whose relationship was said by the Government to be on all fours with other oil companies.[134]

This analogy with private industry must not be pushed too far, however. In the case of wholly- or majority-owned companies, the Government will have strategic powers such as the approval of corporate plans and substantial capital expenditure as well as more specific controls over the acquisition and disposal of assets. Such specific controls may also be attached as conditions to the grant of assistance by the Government even though it only has a minority stake[135] or no equity stake at all.[136] Specific conditions may also make provisions about the dividend policy of the company[137] and compliance with the Government's counter-inflation policy.[138]

Such conditions are designed to promote wider policy objectives

[131] H.C. 347 (1971-2), vol.III, Q.3042-3.
[132] H.C. 298 (1967-8), Q.152.
[133] *Ibid.*, App.I.
[134] *Ibid.*, Q.129.
[135] E.g. I.C.I. (see S.I. 1968 No.990).
[136] E.g. Chrysler (see H.C. 104-i (1975-6), p.14). Meriden co-operative (878 H.C. Deb., col.13, Written Answers, July 29, 1974), Kirkby Manufacturing and Engineering Ltd. (886 H.C. Deb., col. 147, Written Answers (February 12, 1974).
[137] E.g. Chrysler, I.C.L., Ferranti (892 H.C. Deb., col.457, May 14, 1975).
[138] E.g. Chrysler, RR71, Govan Shipbuilders (897 H.C. Deb., col.506, Written Answers (August 7, 1975)). In the case of the Meriden co-operative the Minister's consent was necessary for payments in excess of £50 per week to any employee, director or official.

rather than purely commercial considerations. The memorandum of understanding between the N.E.B. and RR71 carries this a step further by providing that in drawing up its long-range and annual plans RR71 shall have regard to locating expansion in development areas and to furthering industrial democracy.[139] The most important issue of the future is how much further this development will be carried, i.e. to what extent publicly-owned companies will be used as instruments of Government policy where this conflicts with commercial considerations. This crucial issue, which has dominated the Government's relationship with the Nationalised Industries, is beginning to appear in relation to wholly-owned companies. Pressures are already being brought on the Government to make British Leyland buy machine tools from British manufacturers, particularly the wholly-owned firm of Alfred Herbert.[140] This raises the opposite problem about which the Expenditure Committee in its report on the motor industry expressed concern namely the possibility of preferential treatment for British Leyland, if its success did not materialise, at the expense of other motor manufacturers in Britain.[141] Undercutting would be one possibility and this remedy has already been in issue in the export field in the case of Govan Shipbuilders when it was alleged that permission was given by the Government to the company for a loss-making tender for ships from Kuwait.[142] Preferential treatment through allocation of Government contracts is another means of helping companies. As we have seen, it has been used quite explicitly to give support to I.C.L. in which there is only a minority public shareholding.

Perhaps the most controversial precedent for the future is the request to Rolls-Royce (1971) Ltd. to cancel its contracts with the Chile Government — a clearly political interference which was at variance with commercial considerations and for which no compensation was paid to the company. Pressures to take similar action in respect of I.C.L's contract with the South African Government failed but pressures on the Government to intervene in the affairs of such companies when their actions are politically controversial is bound to increase. Whether the N.E.B. will act as a buffer and absorb the Government's pressures on its subsidiaries or whether it will act as a conduit-pipe is too early to foretell. Rolls-Royce fought hard for direct access to the

---

[139] This will be expected of all N.E.B. subsidiaries — see *The Guardian,* June 5, 1976.

[140] 909 H.C. Deb., col. 15 and col. 7, Written Answers (April 5, 1976) — contrast 901 H.C. Deb., col. 1633 (December 2, 1975).

[141] H.C. 617 (1974-5), paras. 292-3.

[142] 909 H.C. Deb., col. 14, Written Answers (April 5, 1976). The Public Accounts Committee was not in favour of such tenders, see H.C. 556 (1975-6), para. 28.

Government but this may not be typical of other subsidiaries or of relationships with the subsidiaries of British Shipbuilders.[143] Much depends on the Parliamentary machinery for calling to account both Ministers and the N.E.B. for the activities of its subsidiaries which will be examined in the next chapter.

The Select Committee on Nationalised Industries pinpointed the basic issues when they commented on wholly or partially publicly owned enterprises; 'If they become more typical as forms of public enterprise in this country, they will have to be examined more carefully and an explicit policy developed for them especially in the fields of pricing ..., investment, and the allowance for social factors and issues of national importance. There is also the problem of fair competition between the public and private sections of mixed industries.'[144] The Government will be under increasing pressure and temptation to abandon its arm's-length relationship with these enterprises and to use them as instruments of Government policy. They will then face the same dilemma as in the case of the nationalised industries of how to reconcile social and political considerations with commercial ones. This raises the fundamental question of what is the purpose of public ownership. Accountability to Parliament can profoundly influence the answer to this question.

[143] See Aircraft and Shipbuilding Industries Bill, Standing Committee D, February 17, 1976, col. 955 *et seq.*
[144] H.C. 65 (1973-4), para.102.

CHAPTER SIX

ACCOUNTABILITY TO PARLIAMENT

MOST of the information contained in the preceding chapters has come from Parliament, whether in the form of questions, statements, debates or committee reports. This is some measure of the extent of accountability to Parliament in respect of Government aid to private industry. Whereas in previous chapters it was the substance of the information which was relevant, here it is used to illustrate the mechanisms of Parliamentary control. The same mechanisms were discussed in Chapter I in relation to Parliamentary control over the provision of aid to industry. This chapter will examine their role in monitoring assistance after it has been provided. As the same Parliamentary procedures are used to fulfil both functions, it is not always possible to draw a hard and fast line between them.

QUESTIONS

The Scylla and Charybdis through which the questioner must steer his course are confidentiality and the refusal of the Minister to accept responsibility.

The rock of confidentiality has been worn away a little lately. As we saw in Chapter I individual grants over a certain figure are now published and the terms and conditions of grants have also been revealed in a number of cases. But Ministers have refused to answer questions about whether applications for financial assistance have been received.[1] They have also refused to disclose confidential commercial information such as the financial forecasts of a firm in receipt of aid[2] or its cash requirements[3] or whether it is selling below cost price[4] or the expected out-turn of a particular order.[5] Productivity targets have also been regarded as confidential.[6] In the case of Harland

---

[1] 886 H.C. Deb., col. 146, Written Answers (February 12, 1975).
[2] 885 H.C. Deb., col. 380, Written Answers (February 3, 1975).
[3] 889 H.C. Deb., col. 218, Written Answers (March 27, 1975).
[4] 886 H.C. Deb., col. 426, Written Answers (February 19, 1975).
[5] 911 H.C. Deb., col. 362, Written Answers (May 17, 1976).
[6] 904 H.C. Deb., col. 341, Written Answers (January 29, 1976), cf. H.C. 556 (1975-6), Q. 1202.

and Wolff the Minister regarded the terms and conditions of employment other than the salary of the managing director as confidential.[7]

However, the Minister would in any case disclaim responsibility for a question of this nature on the ground that it falls within the responsibility of the firm itself.[8] This raises the fundamental issue of how far the Minister accepts responsibility for the running of firms which receive financial assistance. There is an obvious analogy with the nationalised industries where Ministers have refused to answer questions on day-to-day matters.[9] This has not, however, prevented the tabling of questions on such matters if they can be twisted into the form of asking the Minister to give a general direction.[10] In the case of firms in which the Government owns all or the majority of shares the Clerk Assistant of the House of Commons told the Nationalised Industries Committee that all questions about the activity of the firm would be in order, but that still leaves the Minister with the discretion not to answer the question.[11] Mr. Orme, the Minister of State for Northern Ireland, made the sweeping statement that Ministers would answer questions about Harland and Wolff when it was fully-owned in contradistinction to the nationalised industries.[12] This assertion is not borne out by the practice of Ministers.

In practice, Ministers have drawn a distinction between those matters for which they accept responsibility and will answer questions and matters which they regard as the responsibility of the firm. The Minister will answer questions about those whom he has appointed as directors[13] but not the reasons for refusing to appoint a particular person.[14] He has declared the salary of the Chairman of Short Bros.[15] but he has refused to give or justify the salary of the Managing Director of British Leyland on the ground that it was not decided by the Government but by the Board.[16] He gave a similar answer in respect of golden handshakes to former directors of Alfred Herbert.[17] These answers are difficult to reconcile.

As we have seen in the preceding chapter, much of the information

---

[7] 890 H.C. Deb., col. 392, Written Answers (April 24, 1975).
[8] 889 H.C. Deb., col. 11, Written Answers (March 24, 1975).
[9] H.C. 393 (1971-2), App. 9.
[10] H.C. 371-II (1967-8), p.473 *et seq.*
[11] *Ibid.*, Q.1702-7.
[12] 896 H.C. Deb., col. 2483 (August 1, 1975).
[13] 883 H.C. Deb., col. 9, Written Answers (December 9, 1974), and 422 H.C. Deb., col. 119, Written Answers (May 9, 1946).
[14] 847 H.C. Deb., col. 288, Written Answers (December 4, 1972).
[15] 911 H.C. Deb., col. 462, Written Answers (May 18, 1976).
[16] 911 H.C. Deb., col. 935 (May 17, 1976).
[17] 911 H.C. Deb., col. 463, Written Answers (May 18, 1976).

about the relationship between the Minister and a wholly- or partly-owned firm, as well as the arrangements for monitoring, has been contained in answers to Parliamentary questions. It is when M.Ps want to ask about specific issues concerning a firm in which the Government has an interest that problems arise.

Consistent with their refusal to get involved in the management of such firms, Ministers have answered questions on such matters by saying they were the responsibility of the firm. This has been the stock answer to questions about B.P.[18] It was also the answer to a question about I.C.L's sale of a computer to South Africa.[19] In the case of British Leyland the Minister has refused responsibility for its overseas investment policy,[20] the closure of its Italian subsidiary Innocenti[21] and production lost through strikes.[22] He has also disclaimed responsibility for the timing of dismissals by a wholly-owned shipbuilding firm when it closed down Greenwell Dry Dock[23] but he explained that this was done only after confirmation by an independent firm of accountants.[24] He has also answered questions about the number of employees, workloads and salaries in wholly-owned firms.[25] Where he has himself intervened as in the case of Rolls-Royce's contracts with Chile he has of course answered questions on the matter.[26]

The problem with questions about firms in which the Government has a financial interest is not to get them tabled but to get them answered. It is not difficult for a Minister to avoid answering them either on the ground that confidential commercial information cannot be disclosed or that the matter falls within the responsibility of the firm. By this means he can wash his hands of controversial decisions and refuse to justify them but, on the other hand, he can, as in the case of the Chilean contracts, intervene. If this becomes known he must then answer questions unless he can plead confidentiality, but this will not necessarily happen if the 'lunch-table directive' is used as in the case of the nationalised industries. Conversely Parliamentary questions, which are often the expression of outside pressures, may stimu-

[18] 537 H.C. Deb., col. 1867 (March 1, 1955), and 545 H.C. Deb., col. 1996 (November 10, 1955).
[19] 861 H.C. Deb., col. 50, Written Answers (October 16, 1973).
[20] 904 H.C. Deb., col. 543, Written Answers (February 3, 1976).
[21] 901 H.C. Deb., col. 544, Written Answers (December 2, 1975).
[22] 902 H.C. Deb., col. 675, Written Answers (December 17, 1975).
[23] 910 H.C. Deb., col. 24, Written Answers (April 26, 1976).
[24] 908 H.C. Deb., col. 362, Written Answers (March 29, 1976).
[25] 903 H.C. Deb., col. 620, Written Answers (January 23, 1976), and 904 H.C. Deb., col. 101, Written Answers (January 26, 1976). Cf. 925 H.C. Deb., col.92, Written Answers (February 1, 1977).
[26] 874 H.C. Deb., col. 891, Written Answers (June 4, 1974).

late Ministerial intervention as in the case of Cable & Wireless[27] and the statement on political payments by B.P.[28]

The main weakness of Parliamentary questions, as in the case of the nationalised industries, is that when the Minister disclaims responsibility and refuses to intervene they cannot reach the firm concerned. The problem is accentuated by the creation of holding companies such as the N.E.B. Not only does it raise similar problems as the nationalised industries so far as questions about the N.E.B. itself are concerned, but it also raises another barrier between the M.P. and its subsidiaries. As a result of M.Ps concern over this problem,[29] the Leader of the House issued a statement on the matter.[30] Having assured M.Ps that the particular question at issue about numbers and grades of staff of the N.E.B. was a matter of day-to-day management, he then drew attention to the Minister's power to give specific, as well as general, directions and lay down guidelines — all of which could be the subject of questions. He then continued: 'My right honourable Friend will also, within the well-understood limits imposed by the need to maintain necessary commercial confidentiality, be answerable to the House on aspects of the Board's day-to-day management that raise issues of urgent public importance or concern national statistics. He will also be answerable, as appropriate, for the activities of the Board in its capacity as a holding company, particularly in the case of wholly-owned or controlled companies ...' Since this statement was made, the Minister has said that applications and grants for stockbuilding of machine tools, for which the N.E.B. is providing money, are a matter for the N.E.B.[31] and when questioned about the management of subsidiaries[32] has referred to the N.E.B.'s responsibility as well as that of the firm. It does seem, therefore, that M.Ps were justified in regarding the N.E.B. as another barrier between themselves and the firm concerned and a shield with which the Minister can deflect questions from himself. The same is true of the other agencies and public corporations which have been set up in this field.

DEBATES

We are not here concerned with the debates on legislation or Statutory Instruments or resolutions which give Parliamentary approval to

[27] 886 H.C. Deb., col. 201, Written Answers (February 13, 1975).
[28] 911 H.C. Deb., col. 1213 (May 18, 1976).
[29] 901 H.C. Deb., col. 1053 (November 27, 1975).
[30] 902 H.C. Deb., col. 1656 (December 18, 1975).
[31] 912 H.C. Deb., col. 748, Written Answers (June 10, 1976).
[32] 904 H.C. Deb., col. 543, Written Answers (February 3, 1976), and 911 H.C. Deb., col. 463, Written Answers (May 18, 1976). See also 922 H.C. Deb., col. 677 *et seq.* (December 9, 1976).

the provision of aid as these were discussed in Chapter I. As we saw there, two aluminium smelters were debated as the assistance was provided by Statutory Instruments made under the Industrial Expansion Act 1968, which needed the approval of the House. The third smelter, which was coal-fired and did not receive assistance under the 1968 Act, was discussed on the adjournment of the House at the end of the day.[33] Though the latter debate was shorter and had no legal significance, it performed the same political function as the other two debates. The line between Parliamentary approval and Parliamentary accountability is particularly fine here.

Adjournment debates are one of the most frequently used devices for holding the Government to account. As we saw, this was the method used by a backbencher to obtain the only debate on Concorde in 1962.[34] It was also used for a debate on the H.S.146 project.[35] Adjournment debates take place not only at the end of the day but also before the recess when a whole day is set aside for a series of adjournment debates. The motor cycle industry was the subject of such a debate before the summer recess of 1975 to protest against the Minister's withdrawal of support.[36] By challenging the motion fixing the dates for adjournment and reassembly, M.Ps were able to have a short debate on the giving of assistance to two workers' co-operatives as well as other matters which they thought should have been debated before the recess.[37] One of the adjournment debates before the Christmas recess in 1974 was again concerned with assistance given to the co-operative at Meriden.[38] The assistance given to this co-operative was also raised on a point of order because it was feared that assistance would exceed £5 million without Parliamentary approval being obtained.[39] It was raised again later that day on an unsuccessful application for the adjournment of the House under S.O.9.[40]

The assistance given to workers' co-operatives featured again in debates on the second reading of Consolidated Fund Bills which are reserved for a series of debates initiated by backbenchers on the lines of adjournment debates.[41] Assistance to W. & C. French Ltd. was similarly the subject of such a debate[42] as was the N.E.B.[43] Backbenchers'

[33] DELL, *op. cit.*, p. 119.
[34] 669 H.C. Deb., col. 1627 (December 21, 1962).
[35] 883 H.C. Deb., col. 970 (December 12, 1974).
[36] 897 H.C. Deb., col. 734 (August 7, 1975).
[37] 878 H.C. Deb., col. 50 (July 29, 1974).
[38] 883 H.C. Deb., col. 2058 (December 20, 1974).
[39] 878 H.C. Deb., col. 481 (July 30, 1974).
[40] *Ibid.*, col. 495.
[41] 882 H.C. Deb., col. 1699 (December 4, 1974), and 884 H.C. Deb., col. 2050 (January 23, 1975).
[42] 896 H.C. Deb., col. 2412 (July 31, 1975).
[43] 907 H.C. Deb., col. 1653 (March 18, 1976).

motions, for which a number of Fridays are reserved, may also be used for discussing such topics.[44]

The Opposition may also devote a Supply Day to criticising the Government's policy of assistance to industry. After the announcement of aid to Chrysler, the Opposition used a Supply Day to criticise Government aid to the motor vehicle industry.[45] They used another Supply Day to debate this issue on a motion to reduce the Minister's salary.[46] The Government were defeated on this motion due to a technical hitch so that there was another opportunity to debate the issue on a Government motion to restore the status quo.[47] The Opposition may also take the opportunity to divide the House on the Government's policy towards industry by moving an amendment to the address on the Queen's speech on a day when this issue is being debated.[48] The Government may provide time for a debate as they did in the case of U.C.S. after announcing its liquidation.[49] On two occasions there were debates on assistance under the Industry Act 1972 when orders to increase the limit on financial assistance under s.8 were laid before the House for approval.[50] Another opportunity is provided in the annual debate on the reports of the Public Accounts Committee, which increasingly concerns itself with Government aid to private firms.[51] The same applies to debates on the reports of other committees which concern themselves with this question.[52]

These are only some of the ways in which these questions may be discussed on the floor of the House. They may also arise incidentally in the course of a debate on a wider subject. Thus, the rescue of U.C.S. was announced by the Secretary of State in the course of a debate on employment on a Supply Day.[53] The annual debates on the Public Expenditure White Paper may also touch on such questions. So far as Scotland is concerned there is ample opportunity to discuss assistance to Scottish Industry in the Scottish Grand Committee, e.g. in debates on the Scottish Estimates.[54]

---

44 E.g. 827 H.C. Deb., col. 1687 (December 10, 1971), for a debate on public ownership.
45 902 H.C. Deb., col. 1189 (December 16, 1975).
46 905 H.C. Deb., col. 461 (February 11, 1976).
47 905 H.C. Deb., col. 1135 (February 17, 1976).
48 880 H.C. Deb., col. 700 (November 4, 1974).
49 819 H.C. Deb., col. 233 (June 15, 1971).
50 886 H.C. Deb., col. 1267 (February 18, 1975), and 904 H.C. Deb., col. 173 (January 26, 1976). The Industry (Amendment) Act 1976, containing new financial limits, provided further opportunities for debate.
51 E.g. 884 H.C. Deb., col. 49 (January 13, 1975).
52 E.g. see 777 H.C. Deb., col. 1181 (February 11, 1969), for a debate on the Report of the Select Committee on Nationalised Industries (H.C. 298 (1967-8)) concerned with extending its terms of reference to include companies in which the Government has a controlling interest.
53 832 H.C. Deb., col. 50 (February 28, 1972).
54 See Scottish Grand Committee, July 11, 1967, col. 229.

REPORTS AND ACCOUNTS

Accountability to Parliament is also ensured by statutory provisions requiring reports and accounts to be laid before Parliament. The Industrial Development Act 1966,[55] the Industrial Expansion Act 1968[56] and the Local Employment Act 1972[57] all provided for annual reports by the Minister on the discharge of his functions under the Act to be laid before Parliament. The Industry Act 1972 similarly provides for an annual report by the Secretary of State relating to his functions under that Act, the Local Employment Act 1972 and the Shipbuilding Industry Act 1967 to be laid before Parliament.[58] As well as giving total amounts of assistance by area and type of aid, it mentions the names of the recipients in large cases.

Where independent agencies have been set up to provide assistance, similar provisions for reports to Parliament have been made. In the case of the Shipbuilding Industry Board,[59] the Industrial Reorganisation Corporation[60] and the National Enterprise Board,[61] the statutes provide for an annual report to the Minister who shall lay it before Parliament. In each case the reports must set out any directions from the Minister to the Board and in the two former cases, but not with regard to the N.E.B., there were express provisions for stating the grants and loans made and shares acquired by the Board.

The accounts of the I.R.C. were audited by professional auditors and they had to be appended to the annual report together with the auditors' report.[62] The N.E.B. is also made subject to a professional audit and the accounts, together with any report by the auditors, must be laid before Parliament by the Secretary of State.[63] In the case of the S.I.B. and Scottish and Welsh Development Agencies, however, the accounts have to be audited by the Comptroller and Auditor General. This has important implications for accountability to Select Committees which are probably the most effective mechanism for Parliamentary control.

---

[55] Section 12.
[56] Section 7.
[57] Section 17.
[58] Section 16.
[59] Shipbuilding Industry Act 1967, s.8.
[60] Industrial Reorganisation Corporation Act 1966, s.9.
[61] Industry Act 1975, Schedule 2, para. 8.
[62] Industrial Reorganisation Corporation Act 1966, ss. 8 and 9(4).
[63] Industry Act 1975, Sch.2, para. 7.

SELECT COMMITTEES

Public Accounts Committee

If a body is subject to the audit of the Comptroller and Auditor General it will be subject to examination by the Public Accounts Committee and it did make a report on the S.I.B.[64] Where the accounts have to be laid before Parliament, though not subject to the audit of the Comptroller and Auditor General, they fall within the Committee's terms of reference[65] but it will only rarely examine such accounts.[66] Though the I.R.C. was subject to professional audit, the Select Committee on Nationalised Industries as well as the Treasury felt that it came within the Public Accounts Committee's traditional field because receipts into and payments out of the Exchequer in respect of the Corporation were subject to the audit of the Comptroller and Auditor General.[67] They added the proviso, however, that if the I.R.C. were to become self-financing it would no longer be regularly in receipt of public money and fall outside the traditional field of the Public Accounts Committee. The same considerations apply to the N.E.B. which is subject to similar auditing provisions as the I.R.C. in respect of sums provided by the Secretary of State.[68]

The same is also true with respect to the companies in which the Government holds all or some of the shares. Their accounts are not subject to the audit of the Comptroller and Auditor General, though the Department is of course accountable for the expenditure of public money. Thus, B.P. would not fall within the Committee's terms of reference but the Committee has examined many cases where the Government has provided assistance to firms starting with Short Brothers and Harland[69] and Beagle Aircraft,[70] and continuing with Rolls-Royce,[71] Harland and Wolff,[72] U.C.S.,[73] Govan Shipbuilders,[74] Cammell Laird Shipbuilders,[75] the co-operatives and later cases of Govern-

---

[64] H.C. 185-I (1968-9).

[65] S.O. 86.

[66] See H.C. 298 (1967-8), para. 18. Report of Select Committee on Nationalised Industries on its terms of reference.

[67] *Ibid.*, para. 29 *et seq.*

[68] Industry Act 1975, Sch.2, paras. 2(3) and 5(4). The Department's accounting officer is responsible to the Comptroller and Auditor General for money voted to the N.E.B. (906 H.C. Deb., col. 888, March 1, 1976); see further below.

[69] H.C. 647 (1966-7), para. 66.

[70] H.C. 300-I (1970-1).

[71] H.C. 447 (1971-2), para. 14 *et seq.*, H.C. 303 (1974), para. 21 *et seq.*, and H.C. 502 (1974-5), para. 1 *et seq.*

[72] H.C. 447 (1971-2), para. 8 *et seq.*

[73] *Ibid.*, para. 1 *et seq.*

[74] H.C. 374 (1974-5), para. 62 *et seq.*, and H.C. 556 (1975-6), para. 25 *et seq.*

[75] *Ibid.*, and H.C. 374 (1974-5), para. 66 *et seq.*

ment aid.[76] In their report on U.C.S. the Chairman refused to restrict the questioning strictly to the time covered by the Appropriation Accounts because they wanted to see the picture as a whole but the Committee will not examine particular cases in detail until the accounts of the year in which they appear are under scrutiny.[77]

In none of these inquiries did the Committee call representatives of the firms before them, though the Committee have in exceptional circumstances examined private firms as happened in the cases of Ferranti[78] and Bristol Siddeley.[79] The weakness of this procedure was pointed out by Mr. Kenneth Clarke in the debate on the Committee's report of 1971 when he questioned 'whether the Committee of Public Accounts as at present constituted can get behind the ideas and the performance of particular companies to see their motivation. . . We questioned the accounting officers of the various Departments but we were rarely capable of being able to go behind the scenes, as it were, and to get the observations of the concerns which the Government are subventing.'[80] A similar point was made in a debate on the Committee's Reports of 1974 by Mr. Costain who asked, 'As we develop these procedures, should we not also consider including other people to give evidence particularly consultants employed by the Government?'[81]

The Committee have also examined Government assistance to industry under the Industry Act 1972, in general, looking at both the machinery and criteria for giving assistance and the monitoring of firms who have received aid by the Department.[82] Again, no individual firms were called before the Committee. On the contrary, the names of two firms who went into liquidation after receiving Government aid were treated as confidential by the Committee.[83] Similarly, in another case which the Committee examined in depth and where they were critical of the provision of assistance, the name of the company was not divulged.[84] In the case of a firm in Northern Ireland where there were dealings to keep the firm in operation,[85] the Permanent Secretary of the Department of Commerce for Northern Ireland relied on the practice of the Department not to disclose information about

---

[76] H.C. 584 (1975-6), para. 6 *et seq.*
[77] H.C. 374 (1974-5), Qs. 458 and 471.
[78] H.C. 183 (1963-4).
[79] H.C. 571 (1966-7) and H.C. 192 (1967-8).
[80] 827 H.C. Deb., col. 716 (December 2, 1971). For the same point made in a slightly different context, see 847 H.C. Deb., cols. 1726 and 1738 (December 7, 1972).
[81] 884 H.C. Deb., col. 89 (January 13, 1975).
[82] H.C. 303 (1974), para. 41 *et seq.*, and H.C. 374 (1974-5), para. 49 *et seq.* For an earlier investigation of investment grants, see H.C. 166-I (1969-70).
[83] H.C. 303 (1974), Q. 143, p.26.
[84] H.C. 374 (1974-5), Q.509 *et seq.*
[85] H.C. 304 (1974), Q.514 *et seq.*

individual companies with whom they had agreements under industrial development legislation without their consent. Though the terms of the agreement imposed confidentiality on the firm, the practice was to treat the confidence as mutual where it was an on-going operation. After some deliberation the Committee decided to respect this understanding and though they referred to the companies by name themselves these were not published. Mr. Powell, in the debate on the report, criticised the principle of anonymity where big sums of public money were expended in this way and pointed out that anyone in the know would have little difficulty in identifying the firm.[86] As we have seen, there has been a trend towards publishing the names of companies receiving assistance above a fairly low limit and this problem may no longer arise in future though the details of agreements are not published as a matter of course.

The failure to name firms receiving assistance is only one aspect of the wider question of confidentiality. The Public Accounts Committee, unlike the other committees operating in this area, hear evidence in private and publish it with their report. It is, therefore, possible to ask the Committee not to publish confidential evidence by side-lining it and they may accede to such a recommendation. On this basis the Committee may be given confidential information which is not divulged to other committees. Thus, the Public Accounts Committee were given in confidence information about the Government's sales estimates for Concorde and the amount of levy included in the sale price towards the recovery of development costs.[87] This information was denied to the Expenditure Committee when it examined Concorde in the course of its investigation into 'Public Money in the Private Sector.'[88] Mr. Benn later published the relevant figures in a statement to the House.[89] Similarly, the Public Accounts Committee were given in confidence the cost-per-job figure which the Department uses when giving selective assistance under the Industry Act 1972.[90] It is interesting that in 1962 the equivalent figure for assistance under the Local Employment Act 1960 was given to the Estimates Committee without any condition of confidentiality.[91]

Suggestions have been made for televising the proceedings of this Committee[92] but, as has been pointed out,[93] this might prevent the

[86] 884 H.C. Deb., col. 66 (January 13, 1975).
[87] H.C. 335 (1972-3), paras. 57 and 62.
[88] H.C. 347 (1971-2), para. 84 *et seq.,* and App., p. 603.
[89] 870 H.C. Deb., col. 673 (March 18, 1974).
[90] H.C. 303 (1974), Q.160, p.30.
[91] H.C. 229 (1962-3) at p.47.
[92] 903 H.C. Deb., col. 1570 (January 22, 1976).
[93] *Ibid.,* col. 1579.

Committee from receiving confidential evidence as at present, though they could go into private session to hear such evidence as has been done by the Select Committee on Science and Technology[94] and the Expenditure Committee.[95] Apart from the issue of confidentiality, however, television would radically affect the functioning of the Committee which at the moment generally only hear evidence from civil servants.

This is to some extent symptomatic of the difference in emphasis between their reports and those of other Select Committees which is best illustrated by comparing their reports with those of the Expenditure Comittee on the same subject-matter.

Expenditure Committee

There is considerable overlap between the reports of the Public Accounts Committee on Concorde, Rolls-Royce, U.C.S. and Government assistance under the Industry Act 1972 and the Expenditure Committee Reports on 'Public Money in the Private Sector,'[96] 'Regional Development Incentives,'[97] 'The Motor Vehicle Industry'[98] and 'Public Expenditure on Chrysler U.K. Ltd.'[99] but there are also important differences of orientation. The Public Accounts Committee's investigation of Concorde was a very detailed investigation of the reasons for its escalation, its monitoring and the financial arrangements for its production, whereas the Expenditure Committee looked at the Concorde project, Rolls-Royce and U.C.S. as particular illustrations of the general problems of the objectives, the mechanism and the control of Government assistance to private industry. The Expenditure Committee, therefore, has a much wider policy perspective than the Public Accounts Committee, which is concerned more with evolving principles for monitoring of public expenditure rather than its broader objectives. This is again apparent from the reports concerned with the Industry Act 1972. Both Committees took evidence from the Department about the mechanism and criteria for giving aid. The Public Accounts Committee also heard evidence about the arrangements for monitoring which had by then been put into operation. But the Expenditure Committee in its inquiry into regional development incentives was mainly concerned to discover to what extent regional

---

[94] H.C. 621-II (1970-1), Q.916 *et seq.*
[95] H.C. 617 (1974-5), App. III
[96] H.C. 347 (1971-2).
[97] H.C. 85 (1973-4).
[98] H.C. 617 (1974-5).
[99] H.C. 596 (1975-6).

incentives in fact achieved the purposes for which they were designed namely to provide jobs in the development areas.

The Committee started breaking new ground with its inquiry into the motor vehicle industry.[100] It was attracted to the subject by the increasing involvement of the British Government in the industry and started taking evidence shortly after the granting of interim assistance to British Leyland. It examined the Leyland management both before and after the Ryder Report as well as examining Lord Ryder and his team of whose recommendations it was highly critical. It also examined both the Department and the management about Aston Martin's application for aid which had been refused but whilst negotiations were still proceeding. Though in his opening statement the Chairman of the Committee drew attention to the power to make interim reports[101] and it was urged to make such a report by the Chairman of Aston Martin,[102] the report hardly mentioned Aston Martin and was published after the British Leyland Bill became law. The report was a detailed critique of the British motor industry as a whole and the rescue of British Leyland in particular.

The investigation into assistance to Chrysler was the natural corollary of this report. The Committee was not pleased with the Government's reply to its previous report which was contained in an annex to a survey of the British motor vehicle industry and which it felt ignored some of its most important remarks.[103] Aid to Chrysler was certainly not within the spirit of the report and the Committee wanted to examine the Chrysler agreement as a set piece of Government assistance. The Chairman in his opening remarks emphasised that the money had not yet been spent and that the Expenditure Committee as a 'value-for-money' Committee should not wait with its inquiry until the money had been spent. Though the timing of the Expenditure Committee is, therefore, different from the Public Accounts Committee, who could not have examined the issue until the following session, even the Expenditure Committee was in effect conducting a post mortem on how the decision was reached from which lessons for the future could be drawn.

It is not, therefore, so much the timing as the approach of the Expenditure Committee which distinguishes it from the Public Accounts Committee. It is much more concerned with matters of policy than detailed financial control and sets the latter in the context of the former rather than examining it as an end in itself. The difference

---

[100] H.C. 617 (1974-5).
[101] H.C. 617-I (1974-5), Q.1.
[102] H.C. 617-I (1974-5), p.106.
[103] H.C. 104-i (1975-6), Q.1.

in approach of the two Committees is epitomised in their methods of operation. As we have seen, the Public Accounts Committee limits itself almost exclusively to examining civil servants in private at Westminster, whereas the Expenditure Committee examines in a blaze of publicity, if necessary outside Westminster, Ministers and a wide range of witnesses from industry including the main protagonists in the cases under investigation. This can give rise to problems as was the case in the Chrysler investigation.

The Expenditure Committee has the power to require the attendance of witnesses[104] and it has not hesitated to draw this to the attention of firms where it thought it necessary, as in the case of the inquiry into the wages paid to Africans by British firms in South Africa.[105] But it can exercise no compulsion over those not subject to its jurisdiction so that, in its Chrysler inquiry, it had to be content to examine the European Executive Vice-President and the British managers rather than the American chairman.[106] The Chairman of the Committee, with an obvious reference back to the South African inquiry, has also warned witnesses not to give stalling replies.[107] On the other hand the Committee, in its inquiry into Regional Development Incentives, found that firms were prepared to divulge information about assistance which had not previously been published and which the Department at that time treated as confidential.[108]

The other problem encountered by the Committee in its Chrysler inquiry was over the attendance of Mr. Lever, the Chancellor of the Duchy of Lancaster, who had taken a prominent part in the negotiations. Ministers regularly appear before the Expenditure Committee and Mr. Davies gave evidence about U.C.S.,[109] Mr. Benn about Aston Martin[110] and Mr. Varley about Chrysler.[111] But the Prime Minister refused to allow Mr. Lever to appear before the Committee because he had no Ministerial responsibility for the matter.[112] If the Committee had insisted on its right to call the Minister it would have had to report the matter to the House who could have ordered him to attend.[113] In fact the Committee contented itself with trying to discover Mr. Lever's

---

[104] S.O. 87.
[105] H.C. 21-I (1973-4), App., p.90.
[106] H.C. 104-iii (1975-6), Q.445 *et seq.*, Mr. Riccardo was not invited to appear: see H.C. 596-I (1975-6), para. 10.
[107] H.C. 617-I (1974-5), Q.1.
[108] H.C. 85 (1973-4), paras. 133 and 175.
[109] H.C. 347-II (1971-2), Q.2988 *et seq.*
[110] H.C. 617-I (1974-5), Q.569 *et seq.*
[111] H.C. 104-i (1975-6), Q.1 *et seq.*
[112] 903 H.C. Deb., col. 577 (January 15, 1976).
[113] 904 H.C. Deb., col. 1000 (February 2, 1976).

part in the negotiations by questioning Mr. Varley[114] and Sir Peter Carey, the permanent head of the Department,[115] and the Second Permanent Secretary to the Treasury.[116]

Specialist Committees

Some of the specialist committees also have a role to play in investigating Government assistance to industry and again there can be an overlap with other committees. Thus, the Scottish Affairs Committee examined Mr. Benn about U.C.S. immediately after one crisis had been overcome in the course of its inquiry into Economic Planning in Scotland.[117]

There is, however, no overlap so far as the investigation of I.C.L. is concerned. The Science and Technology Committee is the only Select Committee which has so far examined this firm which is receiving £67 million of public money.[118] It took evidence from the firm in the course of its major inquiry into 'Prospects for the U.K. Computer Industry in the 1970's'[119] and again in its follow-up inquiry to consider the extent to which its recommendations had been implemented.[120] The Committee has also taken evidence from Ministers about the Government's relationship with I.C.L.[121] The concern of the Committee in its inquiries has been to look at assistance to I.C.L. in the context of aid to the U.K. computer industry as a whole as well as to investigate the Government's capacity to monitor this huge investment of public money. It, therefore, performs a function analogous to that of the Expenditure Committee in this area.

Select Committee on Nationalised Industries

The gap in coverage left by all these Select Committees is the self-financing firm which is wholly-or partly-Government-owned. Unless like I.C.L. it falls within the ambit of a particular specialist committee, the Public Accounts Committee and the Expenditure Committee will be concerned so long as there is expenditure of public money but when the firm is self-sufficient or profitable it does not fall within the regular supervision of these Committees. It was to fill this gap that the Select

---

[114] H.C. 104-i (1975-6), Qs. 49 *et seq.*, 108, 175 *et seq.*
[115] H.C. 104-ii (1975-6), Qs. 258 and 351.
[116] H.C. 104-ix (1975-6), Q.2050-1.
[117] H.C. 397 (1968-9), Q.1410 *et seq.*
[118] 913 H.C. Deb., col. 269, Written Answers (June 17, 1976).
[119] H.C. 621-II (1970-1), Q.845.
[120] H.C. 97-I (1972-3).
[121] H.C. 621-II (1970-71), H.C. 63-i (1973-4) and H.C. 199-i (1974).

Committee on Nationalised Industries recommended that bodies over which the Government can exercise control should be added to its terms of reference.[122] The Government strongly objected to making B.P. subject to investigation by the Select Committee on the ground that this would tarnish its image of independence abroad.[123] But B.P. did give evidence to the Committee during its inquiry into the Exploitation of North Sea Oil and Gas and it was then questioned about its relationship with the Government.[124] Though probably more brief, this was the sort of questioning that the Committee had in mind when it recommended that the firm should fall within its terms of reference.[125] The Government were equally opposed to other commercial concerns, such as Short Brothers and Harland Ltd., being examined by the Committee on the ground that these were treated by analogy to the private sector and that the Minister would be driven to intervene more if these firms were subject to supervision by the Select Committee.[126] The Committee met these arguments by pointing out that, when examining the nationalised industries, it was not concerned with their day-to-day affairs but with the relationship between them and the Minister.[127] It also pointed out that, in the case of B.P., it would only be concerned with the Government's power *vis a vis* the firm and if the veto power continued never to be used it would give the selection of B.P. a very low priority.[128] The only concession which the Government made to the Committee's views was to add Cable and Wireless Ltd. to its terms of reference,[129] though in evidence to the Commitee the Minister had maintained that this would shatter its independent image abroad.[130]

Mr. Benn also objected to the Committee drawing the line according to whether the Government had an equity shareholding.[131] He argued that this could lead to Ministers using other methods of financing to which the Committee retorted that this would involve an examination by the Public Accounts and Expenditure Committees.[132] With hindsight it is paradoxical that Mr. Benn should have put forward this suggestion as he has argued strongly in favour of an equity shareholding where public money is given to a firm to enable the taxpayer to share in the profits and to ensure public accountability.[133] As we have

[122] H.C. 298 (1967-8), para. 116 *et seq.*
[123] *Ibid.,* Q. 102 *et seq.*
[124] H.C. 345 (1972-3), Q.575 *et seq.*
[125] H.C. 298 (1967-8), para. 70.
[126] *Ibid.,* Q.132 *et seq.*
[127] *Ibid.,* para. 12,and Qs. 156 and 158.
[128] *Ibid.,* para. 70 *et seq.*
[129] 777 H.C. Deb., col. 1181 *et seq.* (February 11, 1969).
[130] H.C. 298 (1967-8), Q.224 *et seq.*
[131] *Ibid.,* Q.159.
[132] *Ibid.,* para. 102.
[133] 886 H.C. Deb., col. 944 (February 17, 1975).

seen, the existence of a Government shareholding does not necessarily ensure greater public accountability. As Mr. Benn himself told the Committee, the Government's relations with wholly- or partly-owned companies are modelled on those with private industry, rather than the nationalised industries. It is precisely this relationship which the Committee felt it was the most appropriate Committee to examine. There are obvious analogies between the Government's relationship with mixed companies and that with the nationalised industries. As we saw, the Committee said in a later report: 'If they [mixed enterprises] became more typical as forms of public enterprise in this country, they will have to be examined more carefully and an explicit policy developed for them especially in the fields of pricing . . ., investment, and the allowance for social factors and issues of national importance. There is also the problem of fair competition between the public and private sections of mixed industries.'[134]

CONCLUSION

The establishment of the National Enterprise Board could bring about such an examination. The Board has vested in it the Government's shareholdings in companies other than shipbuilding and those operating in Northern Ireland and overseas like Cable and Wireless Ltd. and B.P. Ltd. If it were made subject to examination by the Select Committee on Nationalised Industries, the latter would be able to investigate its relationship with the Minister and its subsidiaries.

This possibility did not allay the fears of the Public Accounts Committee about the accountability of the N.E.B. and its subsidiaries. As we have seen, the Department is accountable to the Comptroller and Auditor General, and therefore the Public Accounts Committee for moneys voted to the N.E.B., but the accounts of the N.E.B. itself are subject to professional audit, though they have to be laid before Parliament. These provisions are analogous to those for the nationalised industries which have never been examined by the Public Accounts Committee.[135] If this self-denying ordinance *vis a vis* the nationalised industries is applied to the N.E.B., the Committee will no longer be able to concern itself with money made available to the major undertakings which are its subsidiaries by the Department via the N.E.B.[136] The Committee expressed great concern about this and hoped that arrangements would be made to enable it to examine the operation

---

134 H.C. 65 (1973-4), para. 102.
135 H.C. 298 (1967-8), paras. 11 and 18.
136 H.C. 334 (1975-6), Qs. 785 and 1022.

and control of major Government-assisted undertakings in the way it had done hitherto.[137] So far as Rolls-Royce is concerned, launching aid, which is made available directly to the company from the Department, will be subject to the same scrutiny by the Committee as it is now but where it comes via the N.E.B. the Department will not be accountable.[138] A distinction also has to be drawn between the Board's functions under s.3 of the Industry Act 1975, when it is acting under the Minister's direction and as his agent performing his functions under ss. 7 and 8 of the Industry Act 1972 for which it is reimbursed by him, and when it is acting on its own account out of moneys provided by Parliament.[139] In the former case it will be the function of the Accounting Officer of the Department to ensure that there are proper monitoring arrangements being operated by the N.E.B. and for this he must answer to the Committee. Monitoring will, therefore, be done at one remove and the Committee will be one step further away from the operating subsidiaries. It will still be able to examine the Department about the decision to spend money by a direction under s.3 of the 1975 Act but it will not be able to do so in the case of decisions by the N.E.B. when it is acting on its own account as its accounts are not audited by the Comptroller and Auditor General.[140] Similarly, monitoring arrangements will be the N.E.B's responsibility, though theoretically it would be possible for the Secretary of State to give a specific direction about monitoring.[141]

The creation of the N.E.B. highlights the problems of the Public Accounts Committee in monitoring public expenditure by bodies other than Government Departments. As we have seen, even before the N.E.B. came on the scene there was criticism of the limited role played by the Public Accounts Committee in this new realm where public money is disbursed to institutions not under its oversight. It has been suggested by Mr. Garrett, M.P., that: 'Our State auditors should become what they are — top level management consultants to the Legislature, empowered to seek out and report on managerial malfunction wherever it exists among spenders of public funds.'[142] Mr. Howell, M.P.,[143] pointed out the dangers of confusing the roles of

---

[137] *Ibid.,* para. 64. The Government has stated that the N.E.B. will be making available to the Department information which is also to be available to the Public Accounts Committee and the intention is that the Committee will get all the information necessary to scrutinise all funds advanced by the N.E.B. to large industrial companies — 922 H.C. Deb., col. 760 (December 9, 1976).

[138] *Ibid.,* Qs 785 and 6.

[139] H.C. 104-ix (1975-6), Qs. 2010, 2134 and 2147.

[140] H.C. 334 (1975-6), para. 63.

[141] H.C. 104-ix (1975-6), Q.2147.

[142] 884 H.C. Deb., col. 63 (January 13, 1975).

[143] *Ibid.,* col. 92.

watchdog and the executive which is fundamental to the function of Parliamentary committees whose task is to bring pressure on the executive from outside not to usurp its role.

The real weakness of the Public Accounts Committee lies in the growing number of bodies in receipt of public funds which do not fall within its purview. In this respect the N.E.B. has exacerbated the problem as it not only receives public money but can also dispense it to others. Though it will not be subject to scrutiny by the Public Accounts Committee when acting on its own account, it would fall within the terms of reference of the Expenditure Committee which has already examined its chairman in connection with their investigations into the motor vehicle industry.[144] This Committee is, as we have seen, investigating very closely the *raison d'etre* of Government aid to particular firms and industries and its wider policy implications. There is inevitably an overlap with the Public Accounts Committee and Mr. Dell has suggested that the Public Accounts Committee should take over some of the functions of the Expenditure Committee, leaving the latter with the consideration of priorities of Government spending by examining alternatives in great depth.[145] Such a reorganisation of the functions of the two committees could strengthen oversight of the criteria and mechanisms for disbursing and monitoring Government assistance to industry as well as the wider context of public expenditure in which they take place.

Neither Committee has so far concerned itself in depth with the wide issues of the relationship between Government and industry as a result of Government assistance to private industry. The consequences for the motor car industry of the Government's acquisition of British Leyland were adumbrated by the Expenditure Committee at the end of its report on the motor vehicle industry.[146] But there has been no comprehensive analysis of the Government's relationship with firms in which the Government has an interest to parallel the report of the Select Committee on Nationalised Industries on Ministerial Control.[147] This is what the Nationalised Industries Committee hoped to bring about by an extension of its terms of reference to bodies in which the Government had a controlling interest.[148] The creation of the N.E.B. makes its inclusion within the Committee's terms of reference imperative. This would still leave firms like B.P. whose shares are not vested in the N.E.B. and firms where the Government has no

---

[144] H.C. 104-xxii (1975-6).
[145] DELL, *op. cit.*, p.203 *et seq.* See also, DuCann, *The Parliamentarian* (1976), p. 151.
[146] H.C. 617 (1974-5), paras. 292 and 3.
[147] H.C. 371-I (1967-8).
[148] H.C. 298 (1967-8).

equity stake outside its terms of reference. The line would be an arbitrary one as the acquisition of an equity stake depends on political considerations and, as we have seen, may not be crucial to the Government's relationship with the firm concerned. Even if the Nationalised Industries Committee were confined to examining the N.E.B. and its subsidiaries it could start investigating the same issues it has highlighted in connection with the nationalised industries. Of these, the most crucial is the reconciliation of social and commercial considerations which goes to the heart of Government involvement with industry. The Committee's recommendations on this issue *vis a vis* the nationalised industries has had a profound effect on shaping public attitudes towards these industries. Its views on the mixed sector could be equally potent. Even more important would be the inquiry itself. A dispassionate examination of the novel issues raised by the Government's involvement in an increasing number of private firms, the different types of intervention and the wider implications for the Government's relationship with industry is overdue. Other Select Committees have touched on these issues in particular cases but only the Nationalised Industries Committee has seen the underlying problem and can pull together the diverse strands into an examination of the significance of recent developments in the relationship between Government and industry.

CHAPTER SEVEN

CONCLUSION

THE provision of Government assistance to private industry is not a new phenomenon. In 1875 the Government purchased its shares in the Suez Canal, in 1914 it bought a controlling interest in B.P., in 1943 it acquired the share capital of Short's and in 1946 it took over all the remaining shares in Cable and Wireless Ltd. Since then there have been specific Acts providing assistance to particular industries such as cotton, or individual firms or projects such as the Fort William Pulp and Paper Mills, Rolls-Royce, Concorde and most recently British Leyland. But most assistance is now provided under legislation giving wide discretionary powers to Ministers or public bodies such as the Civil Aviation Act 1949, the Science and Technology Act 1965 and the Industry Acts 1972 and 1975. It is this enormous increase in the power of the State to involve itself in private industry that has given rise to the theory that Britain is becoming a corporate state.[1] The essence of corporatism has been defined by two of the protagonists of this theory as *private* ownership and *state* control.[2] It is revealing to test this theory by applying it to the foregoing account of Government assistance to private firms.

Perhaps the most interesting factor to emerge from this analysis is the opposite of corporatism, namely the company state which is the result of constraining the exercise of public powers within the forms of private company law. One consequence of this is the anomalous position of Government directors who may be appointed to the boards of companies whom the Government has assisted whether by the acquisition of equity or otherwise. Such directors cannot under company law look after the public interest rather than the interests of their shareholders and they are generally regarded as having little part to play in monitoring the Government's stake.[3]

Another problem raised by company law for the Government when giving assistance, is s.332 of the Companies Act 1948, which imposes

---

[1] Winkler, 'Law, State and Economy: The Industry Act 1975 in Context,' *British Journal of Law & Society*, 1975, p.103.
[2] Pahl and Winkler, 'The coming corporatism,' *New Society*, October 10, 1974.
[3] H.C. 104-ix (1975-6), Q.2154-5.

liability for the debts of a company on those who knowingly are a party to the carrying on of any business of the company when there is no reasonable prospect of creditors ever being paid. Though the Government takes the view that the section does not bind the Crown, it regards itself as under an obligation to observe the section. It played a part in the Government's decision to meet the debts of Beagle Aircraft Ltd. in full.[4] In the case of Rolls-Royce the Government was also advised that s.332 might apply if further assistance was provided.[5] The Government refused to accept that there were grounds for an action under the section by the liquidator of U.C.S.[6]

In 1972 the Government announced[7] that: '. . . those doing business with a limited liability company in which the Government had a financial interest must act on the assumption that liability for the company's debts will be determined solely in accordance with the normal rules applicable to a limited liability company under the Companies Act, except where the Government undertakes or has undertaken a specific commitment in relation to those debts.' In the case of assistance to two workers' co-operatives it was expressly stated that no further money would be provided[8] and one of these has gone into liquidation. On the other hand, when further aid was provided for Govan Shipbuilders, the successor of U.C.S., it was expressly stated that, if the Government decided to give no further support to the company because its conditions were not met, the Government would ensure that the company was enabled to discharge its outstanding commitments to shipowners and creditors.[9] A similar assurance that the Government would ensure that the firm's obligations were honoured was given in the case of Short Bros. and Harland Ltd. in August 1972.[10] This is very unusual — in most cases creditors are expected to act on the assumption that the Government will not foot the bill.

The most difficult problem arises when the Government is deciding whether or not to grant assistance to a company in financial difficulties. If it grants interim assistance whilst satisfying itself about financial

---

[4] H.C. 447 (1971-2), para. 100 and App. 2.

[5] Report of D.T.I. Investigation, H.M.S.O., 1973, para. 565.

[6] 888 H.C. Deb., col. 473, Written Answers (March 20, 1975).

[7] H.C. 447 (1971-2), Q.1548, and 832 H.C. Deb., col. 282, Written Answers (March 7, 1972).

[8] 878 H.C. Deb., col. 108 (July 29, 1974), and *ibid.*, col. 13, Written Answers. Further assistance has been provided to the Meriden co-operative, see 925 H.C. Deb., col. 1056 (February 7, 1977).

[9] 897 H.C. Deb., col. 508, Written Answers (August 7, 1975).

[10] 842 H.C. Deb., col. 454 *et seq.*, Written Answers (August 9, 1972). A specific commitment was also given in respect of Rolls-Royce (1971) Ltd., see 850 H.C. Deb., cols. 1247-8 (February 13, 1973). See also 822 H.C. Deb., col. 196, Written Answers (July 30, 1971), for a commitment in respect of I.C.L's leasing operations. The N.E.B. guidelines provide that the N.E.B. must have regard to the practice of companies in the private sector in relation to the debts of its subsidiaries.

viability, it is in danger of offending against s.332. It has, therefore, been advised of two alternative possibilities — either to give interim assistance and announce the circumstances in which it is given which will reveal the circumstances of the firm concerned or to give interim aid on terms under which the Department would make good losses caused to any new creditors after the date when the assistance was given and also would make good any additional losses caused to other creditors through continued trading.[11] This latter alternative seems not to have been used to date but there have been a number of cases where interim assistance has been announced.[12] However, revealing the circumstances of the firm concerned has not brought about the very result that the giving of assistance was intended to avoid, presumably because the rescue of the firms concerned was confidently expected. But interim assistance will not always provide a solution and the Government has suggested that an Official Trustee to take temporary responsibility might be desirable.[13] This White Paper proposal was not implemented in the Industry Act 1975, presumably because of the difficult issues of company law involved.

The effect that s.332 may have in inhibiting the Government from giving assistance in certain cases, and possibly in monitoring assistance after it has been provided,[14] is another illustration of how unsuitable it is to apply the Companies Act to a Government providing assistance to a firm in difficulties. But perhaps even more inappropriate is the whole concept of limited liability which the Government reiterated in its statement in 1972. In the debates on the reports of the Public Accounts Committee dealing with the Beagle affair several M.Ps questioned whether this doctrine should apply to the Government. Mr. Paget thought that a company wholly-owned by the Government should have unlimited liability[15] and Mr. John Nott suggested it would be better to run such companies as partnerships.[16] The difficulty would be how far to apply such principles to companies where the Government involvement was less than 100 per cent. Mr. Madden said that he would draw a distinction between Government intervention on a commercial basis, where it should be able to limit its liability, and intervention for social reasons, where its liability should be unlimited.[17] Again, this distinction would be a difficult one to draw.

11 H.C. 303 (1974), Q.118, p.21.
12 E.g. British Leyland, Alfred Herbert, Ferranti.
13 Cmnd. 5710, para. 34.
14 H.C. 447 (1971-2), para. 99, and Q.3121 *et seq.*
15 827 H.C. Deb., col. 699 (December 2, 1971), and 847 H.C. Deb., col. 1709 *et seq.* (December 7, 1972).
16 827 H.C. Deb., col. 698.
17 847 H.C. Deb., col. 1714 *et seq.*

Mr. Lever thought that the extent of the Government's participation in the company's affairs was the crucial factor and drew a distinction between B.P., where creditors would not rely on the Government's shareholding, and those firms where the Government actively intervenes in the affairs of the company where the Government should be liable.[18]

This raises the whole issue of the extent to which the Government participates in the affairs of companies incorporated under the Companies Act and for what purposes. When the articles of association are in accordance with Table A, the management of the company is vested in the directors. Even where the company is wholly-owned by the Government so that as sole shareholder it appoints all the directors it has firmly stated that the board should as far as possible operate as a board of a privately-owned company and the Government would not concern itself with the day-to-day running of the company and would not diminish the responsibility of the board for the management of the company's affairs.[19] The relationship between the Government and the company may be embodied in a directive to the Chairman and directors[20] or guidelines[21] or a memorandum of understanding[22] laying down the areas where Government approval is necessary. This does not prevent, as we saw, interference in individual cases as in the case of Rolls-Royce's contracts with Chile. Such interference may be expected to increase in politically-delicate áreas and in some cases the Government has in its guidelines asked for advance warning of politically-sensitive decisions from the company.[23] But such interference may be in direct conflict with the overall duty imposed on such companies to act on normal commercial principles. The Government will have to resolve this conflict. It might also be more realistic for the Government to recognise, as in the case of some nationalised industries, that a commercial yardstick was not possible in certain cases such as Govan Shipbuilders. It would have been easier and more open for the Government to justify its continued support for the company on the grounds of unemployment rather than the pretence of commercial viability. This would not mean an open-ended commitment any more than subsidies for the nationalised industries are open-ended but it

---

[18]   827 H.C. Deb., cols. 701 and 724.

[19]   E.g. Cmnd. 4817 (1971) and Memorandum between the Government and Rolls-Royce (1971) Ltd., 874 H.C. Deb., col. 299 (June 4, 1974), Written Answers.

[20]   Short Bros. and Harland Ltd., Beagle Aircraft Ltd.

[21]   Cable and Wireless Ltd.

[22]   Rolls-Royce (1971) Ltd.

[23]   Memorandum of Understanding between the N.E.B. and Rolls-Royce (1971) Ltd. and in the case of Cable and Wireless Ltd., see H.C. 472 (1975-6), para. 18 — Report of Select Committee on Nationalised Industries.

would make clear that profit need not be the sole criterion for publicly-owned companies any more than for the nationalised industries.

The position of the Government is much more difficult where it provides assistance to a private firm, whether by loan, grant or the taking of equity. Where the Government owns the majority of the shares, as in the case of Short's, the position is analogous to the wholly-owned company, though the extent to which the Government uses its power will depend very much on the particular company, as is illustrated by its complete abstention from interference in the affairs of B.P.

Where the Government holds a minority stake, the shareholding itself will not confer greater powers than those of any other minority shareholder, but the Government may reserve to itself certain powers as a condition of granting assistance by this method. Thus, the scheme under which assistance was originally provided for I.C.L. required the Minister's approval for certain matters so long as he owned 5 per cent of the shares.[24] The power to appoint a director was also made conditional on the holding of this percentage of shares.[25] But such powers may be conferred irrespective of any shareholding as a condition of obtaining assistance.[26] The controversy about the acquisition of equity in a company is basically a political one but the Government has been criticised from opposite sides of the House on occasions when it has given assistance without acquiring an equity stake. In the case of the co-operatives the Opposition criticised,[27] whereas in the case of Chrysler[28] and Brentford Nylons[29] the criticism came from its own side. In the last case and that of Kearney & Trecker Marwin,[30] the Government's justification was the temporary nature of the intervention but in the case of the co-operatives political considerations must have played an important part whilst in the case of Chrysler an equity stake was not part of the package deal which was finally negotiated. Though political and practical considerations are, therefore, predominant in decisions about the acquisition of equity in return for assistance, Mr. Benn has stressed the aspect of public accountability.[31] However, an equity stake does not *per se* give the Minister greater powers than a private shareholder under the Companies Act. It is the statutory powers under which assistance is given which enable him to attach conditions providing powers of control over the company.

24   S.I. 1968 No. 990, para. 12.
25   Cmnd. 3660, para. 14(b).
26   E.g. Chrysler UK Ltd. and the co-operatives.
27   886 H.C. Deb., col. 1289 (February 18, 1975).
28   902 H.C. Deb., col. 1173 (December 16, 1975).
29   916 H.C. Deb., col. 17 (July 26, 1976).
30   915 H.C. Deb., col. 1441 (July 19, 1976).
31   886 H.C. Deb., col. 944 (February 17, 1975).

The same powers of control may be made a condition of assistance by grant or loan.[32] These have been cited as illustrations of the way in which the corporate state controls the economy by the use of general laws for purposes not explicit in the law itself.[33] This is one aspect of the matter but these conditions are also the only way in which it can be ensured that public money is used for the public benefit. At its lowest the Government must ensure that it will not lose its investment if it is repayable and that the money is used for the purposes for which it was provided. Much more difficult is the monitoring of the objectives for which assistance was given. Thus, in the case of Chrysler, it was made a condition for releasing tranches of loan that in Chrysler's opinion progress was being made towards the Stoke Linwood and Truck Plan and the C6 programme and that satisfactory agreements with the workforce were being concluded. But, as is obvious, this fell short of a binding agreement.[34] It is even more difficult to monitor objectives such as the provision of new employment as a result of assistance.[35] The Government has to rely to a large extent on the reliability of the firm's forecasts and its good faith.[36] Monitoring should reveal any changes from the firm's stated intentions and the need for future assistance is some guarantee of good faith but whether the estimated number of jobs materialises is another matter. Even more speculative is for how many years these jobs will be provided.[37]

Where non-selective assistance, such as investment grants and regional development grants, is provided there can be no guarantee of increased employment. This is illustrated by the closure of Courtauld's factory at Skelmersdale for which investment grants worth millions of pounds were paid.[38] One of the purposes behind planning agreements is to harmonise the company's plans with national objectives and in particular to tailor selective assistance more effectively to national needs. They will not, however, affect the availability of regional development grants. Conditions attached to the grant of assistance to make the firm comply with Government policy on dividends or counter-inflation may be regarded as an embryonic form of planning agreement.

[32]　E.g. Chrysler UK Ltd. and the co-operatives.
[33]　Winkler, *op. cit.*, p.119 *et seq.*
[34]　H.C. 596-I (1975-6), para. 151 *et seq.*
[35]　H.C. 303 (1974), Q.148, p.27.
[36]　H.C. 374 (1974-5), Q.525.
[37]　Pilot surveys of assistance provided under the Local Employment Acts indicated that on average 85-90 per cent of the jobs estimated had been provided three years later but there were wide variations between different projects: H.C. 442 (1971-2), p.3; H.C. 127 (1970-1), para. 24 *et seq.*; and H.C. 559 (1970-1), para. 23 *et seq.*
[38]　H.C. 327 (1972-3), para. 304 *et seq.*; 918 H.C. Deb., col. 741, Written Answers (November 5, 1976); and 919 H.C. Deb., col. 1687 (November 18, 1976). The amount to be repaid because of the closure has still to be determined.

The most effective mechanism by which the Government can exercise control over the assistance it provides to industry is the procurement contract. Winkler cites control by contract as another example of using the law in general, i.e. not explicit in any statute, to control the economy. The power which the Government can exercise through its purchasing policy over a particular firm is illustrated by I.C.L. The Select Committee on Science and Technology pointed out that the consequences of this policy could lead to close involvement of the Government in the affairs of the company.[39] An illustration of the Government's control through contract over an industry is its relationship with the aircraft industry. It was this close relationship which led the Plowden Committee to recommend that the Government should take a stake in the airframe companies.[40] The Government used the same argument to justify nationalisation. On the other hand Mr. Amery, for the Opposition, argued that the control which the Government has over the industry as customer made nationalisation unnecessary.[41] These three solutions represent different ideologies of public ownership but also different degrees of public accountability.

We have seen the difficulties posed by company law for achieving public purposes, which is one aspect of the problem of public accountability. Professor Robson drew a very unfavourable comparison between the public corporation and the joint stock company as forms of public enterprise:[42] 'The joint stock company compares unfavourably with the public corporation in almost every respect. It is not created by Parliament or in any way answerable to it. It is not directly under the control of the Government, except insofar as Ministers can control the membership of the board or influence their policy indirectly. Its activities and policies are sometimes carried on behind a thick smokescreen of secrecy which conceals much of what should be publicly known. Its policy is neither openly laid down in an Act of Parliament after public debate nor are there usually opportunities for discussing it in the Legislature. Its reports and accounts are either not published or are no more informative than those of a commercial undertaking.' Much of this is as true today as when it was written, with the difference that the device is now used much more widely. The same is true of mixed enterprise, i.e. the company in which the Government holds shares to which the same criticisms can be applied. *A fortiori,* they apply to a company in which the Government holds no equity but which it assists with loans or grants or by purchasing its products. The

---

[39] H.C. 309 (1972-3) para. 56.
[40] Cmnd. 2853 (1965) Chap. 37.
[41] 901 H.C. Deb. cols. 1451 and 1484 (December 2, 1975).
[42] W.A. Robson, 'Nationalised Industry and Public Ownership,' 1960, p.28.

most difficult problem raised by the enormous expansion of Government assistance to industry is how to make the firms publicly accountable. Far more attention has been devoted to the problem of making Ministers accountable, for which there exist well-tried mechanisms, even if they are not fully effective. But in the case of limited companies there is a dearth of procedures by which they can be held directly accountable. Public accountability is to and through the Minister or the N.E.B. and there are few opportunities for Parliament, let alone the public, to question firms directly.

Questions in Parliament can only be addressed to Ministers and, as we have seen, they can avoid answering on the ground that they fall within the responsibility of the firm or the N.E.B. Committees of the House can question anyone within the jurisdiction and firms have given evidence directly on matters which fall within the competence of the Select Committees on Science and Technology, Scottish Affairs, Expenditure and Nationalised Industries. But Cable and Wireless Ltd. is the only limited company which has been added to the terms of reference of the Nationalised Industries Committee, though it has taken evidence from B.P. Ltd. in connection with its inquiry into North Sea Oil and Gas.[43] The most outstanding omission is the Public Accounts Committee, which does not hear evidence from firms, though exceptionally it did examine Ferranti and Bristol Siddeley about excessive profits made on Government contracts.[44] If this were to become the norm rather than the exception such firms would be much more closely accountable to Parliament. But even more important would be to widen the jurisdiction of the Comptroller and Auditor General to examine the accounts of firms in receipt of public money. This exists in other countries, particularly the United States of America and Germany.

In the United States the Comptroller General has access to the books and records of Government contractors where contracts are not put out to tender and he carries out what amounts to an efficiency audit which is far in advance of the functions performed by the Comptroller and Auditor General.[45] As we saw above, Mr. Garrett, M.P., recommended extending the jurisdiction of the Comptroller in both these directions.[46]

In Germany the equivalent of the Comptroller and Auditor General *(Bundesrechnungshof)* conducts a super-audit of the accounts of companies in which the Federal Republic holds shares after they have been

43 H.C. 345 (1974-5).
44 H.C. 183 (1963-4), H.C. 571 (1966-7) and H.C. 192 (1967-8).
45 Normanton, 'The Accountability and Audit of Governments', p.178 *et seq.*
46 884 H.C. Deb., col. 63 *et seq.* (January 13, 1975).

audited by a professional auditor and reviewed by the Minister.[47] The purpose of this super-audit is to ensure that the Ministry is performing its functions properly as well as the management. One of its aims has been to see that the Government directors on the boards of the companies are exercising adequate supervision over the management and that the Ministry exercises proper control over its representatives. There are of course fundamental differences between German and English company law and Government directors here have not played an active role on behalf of the Government in the case of companies in which it has a minority stake or where it has provided assistance by other means. Nevertheless, the Comptroller and Auditor General could in the same way as his German counterpart play an important role in overseeing such companies directly as well as the Department's monitoring of the firms.[48]

The German *Bundesrechnungshof* also concerns itself with the Government's policy towards enterprises in which it has a stake, in particular, their profitability. The Public Accounts Committee is increasingly drawn into this field and has recently recommended in the case of Govan Shipbuilders Ltd. and Cammell Laird Shipbuilders Ltd. that the costs of keeping the yards open should be quantified and compared with the estimated social and other costs likely to result from closure.[49] However, the Public Accounts Committee is not perhaps the best body to examine the wider policy issues of the relationship between the Government, the N.E.B. and firms in receipt of assistance. The Nationalised Industries Committee would be far more suitable to investigate this problem, which is closely analogous to the relationship between Ministers and the nationalised industries.

The analogy with the nationalised industries can be extended into the realm of consumer affairs. All the nationalised industries have consumer councils which have been critically examined by the National Consumer Council[50] whose Chairman, Mr. Michael Young, has expressed the hope that the consumer point of view would be represented in companies like British Leyland, B.P., Cable and Wireless or any other company providing goods or services in which the Government has a financial stake. Social Audit Ltd., an independent non-profit making organisation, is concerned with investigating and reporting on the social impact of corporate bodies and to some extent per-

---

[47] Normanton, *op. cit.*, p.354 *et seq.*
[48] Where the N.E.B. holds the equity stake in the firm, there is now an additional barrier between the Public Accounts Committee and the firm — see H.C. 334 (1975-6), para. 59 *et seq.*
[49] H.C. 556 (1975-6), para. 30.
[50] National Consumer Council Report No. 1: 'Consumers and the Nationalised Industries,' H.M.S.O., 1976.

forms the function of a consumer council for such bodies. In its journal *Social Audit* it published allegations about Cable and Wireless which led to an investigation by the Department and which were later examined by the Select Committee on Nationalised Industries.[51]

The allegations by Social Audit Ltd. about Cable and Wireless Ltd. illustrate very well Professor Robson's charge that the activities and policies of companies are 'sometimes carried on behind a thick smoke-screen of secrecy which conceals much of what should be publicly known.'[52] The charges concerned Coltronics Ltd., a company acquired by Cable and Wireless, which, as a result of misconduct by the manager, involved the company in substantial losses. Neither the Department nor the Treasury knew of the extent of Coltronics' losses until the Social Audit report was published. An investigation was then made by the Department and it transpired that the Department had been kept in the dark in the hope that a more satisfactory solution to the affair could be achieved. It was admitted by the company that this was an error of judgment and the guidelines laid down by the Department have been changed so that such circumstances must be reported. The affair was not specifically mentioned in the directors' report because the company were concerned for their good name and the matter did not appear on the face of the accounts for the year in question though it was fully disclosed in the accounts of the following year. It was agreed with hindsight that in the case of a publicly-owned company in this situation it would have been better to disclose the matter in the previous year's accounts. What is perhaps the most frightening aspect of the affair is that the Department were advised that the company had not only complied with the Companies Act but had perhaps done a little more than they need have done. The case shows again the dangers of applying private company law to publicly-owned companies.

Government assistance to industry raises the basic problem of using private bodies for public purposes. The Company or the Contract State is the result. It represents the reverse side of the Corporate State in that it shows the difficulty of making private bodies publicly accountable for the public money they receive and of using private law mechanisms for public ends. Public accountability involves accountability to Ministers, Parliament and directly to the public. Company law puts obstacles in the way of achieving accountability in all three spheres. Because Government directors cannot represent the public interest where it conflicts with the interests of the shareholders, the

[51]   H.C. 472 (1975-6), Chap. VII.
[52]   *Supra*, n.42.

Government has to rely on indirect pressures or other means, such as conditions for contracts and grants of assistance or planning agreements, to ensure that companies use public money for public purposes. Parliament cannot hold companies directly accountable because their accounts cannot be examined by the Comptroller and Auditor General and they are not included within the terms of reference of the Select Committee on Nationalised Industries. Company accounts are too uninformative to ensure accountability to the public. Reforms in these areas would improve the accountability of companies but they would still leave the limited company defective as a vehicle for public ownership. Not only is limited liability out of place in this context but the whole analogy with a privately-owned company is misleading. The companies which are publicly-owned have been directed to act commercially like private companies, which begs the question of what is the purpose of public ownership. As in the case of the nationalised industries the Government has to face this issue.[53] It cannot be evaded by hiding behind the veil of incorporation, even when it is covered by the mantle of the N.E.B.

---

[53] See, 'A Study of U.K. Nationalised Industries,' N.E.D.O. Report, 1976.

INDEX